FINDING
A
PASTOR

DR. JOEL HATHAWAY

FINDING
A
PASTOR

A HANDBOOK FOR
MINISTERIAL SEARCH COMMITTEES

PCA Committee on Discipleship Ministries,
1700 North Brown Road, Suite 102
Lawrenceville, GA 30043

ISBN 978-1-944964-17-7

Library of Congress Information

COVER DESIGN:
Darren Welch Design | darrenwelchdesign.com

INTERIOR DESIGN:
Katie Rhea Stokes Design and Lettering | katierhea.com

TABLE of CONTENTS

INTRODUCTION

A MINISTERIAL SEARCH COMMITTEE is tasked with identifying a spiritual leader with the training and experience requisite for the congregation and context in which he or she will be hired to serve. This is a serious undertaking. The task demands that the committee have a patient humility that is direct and explorative, a capacity for self-reflection and, above all, a dependence upon the Holy Spirit. The process of finding a new pastor will be tumultuous, but it does not have to be traumatic. It is difficult, but does not have to be destructive.

The challenges of hiring, retaining, and sustaining ministry leaders in vocational settings are not primarily challenges of theological discourse or academic expression. The challenges begin with *you*: the individuals chosen by your congregation to participate in or potentially lead a pastoral search process—and they are as much relational, behavioral, and emotional as they are spiritual. How well a search committee understands in the simplest terms the organizational dynamics of its congregation and the committee members' own emotional-behavioral patterns around areas of fear, change, transition, power, and leadership (to name just a few) will impact success or guarantee failure in the pastoral search process.

Larger, more resourced churches looking for professional guidance in the pastoral hiring practice have access to many paid consultants. The process outlined here still applies to these large and complicated organizations. However, this resource was crafted for the majority of churches around the world—those with under 200 attendees. These congregations tend to have fewer resources available, fewer support networks to draw on, and are usually more isolated regionally and denominationally. These churches think of a pastoral search process in more traditional, even parish, terms.

They are less aware of the complex system that places them in a model of knowledge-dependency and system-interconnectivity. More simply put, these churches are less aware of the interplay of organizational styles and personal preferences that can keep them mired in old habits and old ways of thinking.

Our desire is to help these churches grow in spiritual health, emotional awareness, and theological depth, as well as prepare them to hire godly leaders for their various ministry positions—leaders who are broken but redeemed, who use their gifts to serve in largely anonymous ways, who lead their congregations always with both hands pointed to the true head of the church, Jesus Christ. In other words, this resource was written for *you*.

For all these reasons, I have taken great care to craft this guide in terms that any intelligent congregation member can understand. Some may argue that I have simplified it too much, but I do not buy into the notion that to be meaningful one must speak in profound and complex terms. The aim here is to provide practical, real-world assistance to those who will give a great deal of time and energy to the difficult task of identifying and selecting new church leaders. Clarity and concision have thus been my goal.

Finally, the approach described here was developed to allow a search committee to adequately, fairly, and without bias evaluate both internal and external candidates using the same process and criteria. For the sake of the internal candidate and his or her family, and that of the congregation, a search committee's final recommendation on an internal candidate needs to stand up to the same robust test of evaluation as any external candidate.

In what follows, I depend and build upon the long years of experience of Dr. Philip D. Douglass, whose research, teaching, and insights have been formative for my thinking in this area.

PART ONE

The Pastoral Search Committee: People and Process

I. Establishing a Search Committee

DEFINITIONS

As we begin, here's a definition that many would say describes the make-up and purpose of a search committee:

> *A search committee is a collection of individuals (not a "group") elected to a task (not a process) for which they have not been trained: to determine the fitness of one candidate (among many) for a position about which the committee members have minimal experience, limited understanding, and almost no organizational knowledge.*

Let me first expound on the terminology of this definition before considering some of the objections to it that may arise.

- *Collection of individuals* means that the search committee is not a homogenous or cohesive group simply because all the people on the committee have been elected to a common task. The journey toward becoming a cohesive group is a months-long process at best, while the hope of becoming completely homogenous usually goes unrealized.

- **Elected** simply means that most search committees come into existence through a standardized nomination/election process.

- **Task** means that most committees view their job as a task that is limited, definable, process-oriented, and has specific mileposts along the way toward completion. However, in practice the work of a committee is more of an ongoing process involving the development of the committee's own collective identity, a differentiated relationship with the church it represents, and the recognition that the committee's work is less technical than adaptive (that is, more ambiguous, indefinable, varied, and unpredictable), which requires ongoing and active learning.

- **Not trained** means that most committees do not go through an intentional, thorough orientation. Even fewer are trained by skilled practitioners for the process to which they have been elected. Many denominations or individual congregations have bylaws describing the make-up, election, and scope of a search committee. From there, committees are expected to "figure it out as they go." This often involves drawing from similar but imprecise, even non-transferable experience in another industry. For example, committee members who have worked with a corporate human resources team will often assume that their experience in that setting is immediately applicable to the church context.

- **One candidate** means one from among the many potential applicants.

- **Fitness** means that there are capacities, characteristics, and qualities desired in a candidate. However, the identification of these capacities, characteristics, and qualities in one candidate over and against all others requires a process thorough and consistent enough to produce reliable results and dynamic enough to adjust along the way.

- *Position* refers to the role the minister will assume, whether senior, solo, associate, youth, worship, women's, discipleship, or other support role —with all its duties, responsibilities, and expectations, written and unwritten, spoken and unspoken.

- *Minimal experience and limited understanding* means that few if any members on a search committee have ever served in the position for which they are interviewing candidates. This lack of personal experience is a knowledge gap for most committees, leaving them unclear on how daily expectations regularly differ from a clear, defined job description.

- *Organizational knowledge* refers to actual knowledge about the search process from within the committee's church. If a committee performs its process well, it should not have to repeat the process again with any regularity. Thus, a church replacing a pastor after 20 years has little relevant organizational knowledge about how the process was last handled. For most churches, if search committees are formed with regularity, either the committee is unsure of how to manage the process or the process itself is not working to identify best-fit candidates. In either event, the outcome is the same: frequent pastoral turnover.

Common objections to this definition and the need for an identifiable search committee process include statements like the following:

- "We are educated people. We can figure out the process ourselves."
- "We know our church better than anybody on the outside. That makes us the best people for this job."

- "We've done this before. We know what we're doing."
- "Lots of us have helped with hiring in our companies. How is this any different?"
- "This process cannot be that hard."
- "We're trusting the Spirit to guide us along the way."

My assumption is that members of search committees are educated people who know and love their churches, who have practical life experience—and sometimes even technical business experience—who depend upon the leading of the Holy Spirit. If they are lacking in any of these areas, especially in trust of the Spirit, this should be the first concern.

But after working with and studying hundreds of search committees, my experience is that the process is harder and more complex than most committees know. It will take longer than anticipated and stretch members beyond observed experience. It is unlike any other hiring process. The best analogy comes from the family business model. The hired individual will have formal duties and expectations. There will be evaluations and performance feedback. But this person is also part of "the family." He or she will share meals with you, be a guest in your homes, and be invited into the most intimate parts of your lives.

These challenges do not free search committees to adapt a "let go and let God" approach. Because the Holy Spirit is an active member of every pastoral search team, it is all the more important for committees to seek wisdom and understanding, and to develop and adopt best practices for the identification of their next pastor. If you are on a search committee, you are not just helping your congregation to call a pastor. You are helping to call the person who will be one of—if not the most—regular articulators of the gospel in your church, for your family, and to unbelievers yet to receive the gospel of grace. That is no small undertaking.

How has your committee sought to identify its knowledge gaps?

COMMITTEE COMPOSITION

The composition of the committee will reflect your church's theological beliefs, communal values, and organizational practices. Churches that place a higher value on the influence of leadership will tend to put more elders and other elected officers onto a search committee. Churches that practice a robust complementarianism will tend to broaden representation to include non-ordained and non-officer men and women. Still other churches practice a broad egalitarianism.

I specifically want to focus on those committees that hold to a firm complementarianism. Please do not displace, by intent or oversight, the role godly women in the congregation have in the pastoral search committee. Most candidates are called to minister broadly to many ages, to those in various stages of marriage and singleness, and to both men and women. Committees that exclude godly women in the church from advising, serving alongside, and speaking into the ministerial search process are more likely to miss negative emotional, relational, and behavioral indicators expressed by candidates. Women and children are most likely to experience these negative relational realities. If news of the abuse of power in congregations is not enough of a sobering reason to include a diversity of people of spiritual maturity on the search committee, then consider the words of the apostle Paul, who warns against the tendency of those in power to abuse it (see 2 Cor. 11:21).

We recommend that the search committee be composed of five to seven voting members, with representation from:

- the church leaders (e.g., elders or deacons),
- men and women in various roles of service who have informal power in the congregation,
- and a range of members from those who are newer to those who are more established.

All committee members should be growing in sanctification toward spiritual maturity.

More than seven members on a committee makes unanimity less likely. Committees that have more than seven voting members typically establish a threshold of agreement in a more democratic fashion. For example, one church we worked with had nine voting members on the committee, with the written agreement that seven members had to agree on a candidate before he would be asked to visit.

Many committees also have alternative members: one or two people who observe the candidate evaluation process from the very beginning. These people are included in the committee evaluation exercise. They can ask questions and speak to issues throughout the process, and they can become voting members of the committee if a standing member recuses herself or resigns from the committee. Life circumstances—the birth of a baby, a job transition along with a physical move, or health issues—are the main causes of a voting member leaving the committee. Committees are commended to plan for the loss of a committee member by electing alternative, back-up members.

SEARCH PROCESS TIMELINE

The search process will take longer for some churches than for others, depending on a variety of factors that will be outlined in the following pages. In general, the timeline presented here offers a good estimate based on our experience of the time involved for each stage of the process.

MONTHS	ACTION/TASKS
1	Committee formed
2 – 3	Committee Dynamics Exercise
3 – 4	Committee Dynamics Exercise continued / Congregational Survey conducted
5	Congregational Survey evaluated / Job Description (version 1) formed
6 – 7	Interview Best-Fit Candidates / Job Description (version 2) formed
7 – 8	Job Description (version 2) continued / First Candidates: Written Questionnaire, Listen to Sermons
9 – 10	Second Candidates: Written Questionnaire, Listen to Sermons / First Candidates: Phone Interview
11 – 13	Third Candidates: Written Questionnaire, Listen to sermons / Second Candidates: Phone Interview / Eliminate or Decline Candidates
14 – 15	Retained Candidates: Second Interview (video) / Interview References
16 – 17	Retained Candidates: Site Visit / Vote before next candidate visits
18	Job Offered / Accepted

II. The Old Model of Pastoral Hiring

It used to be that when a church needed a new pastor, the congregation elected a search committee, internally generated a job description, mailed it to denominational collecting agencies and local seminaries, and then waited for interested candidates to apply. When enough resume packets arrived, the committee began eliminating some from and advancing others through the process. After the committee narrowed down the pool to a few remaining candidates, some final evaluation took place. This usually included a site visit by each potential candidate. Eventually, when a candidate met most or all the criteria, the committee endorsed the candidate, the congregation voted to accept the candidate, and the church extended a call. Everybody lived happily ever after—except that, more often, they did not.

In 2010, a church south of Denver, Colorado, employed this model. In the Pastoral Profile, announcing the call of the new pastor, the committee shared its process, specifically how it

published the search in a variety of venues and received over 100 inquiries. Of
these, 70 individuals completed the application process. From the 70 applicants, the
committee selected 10 candidates with whom it conducted 45-minute phone inter-
views. From those interviewed, it selected 5 "semi-finalists" with whom the commit-
tee conducted more extensive interviews (by phone and in person), checked references,
and received additional written input. From the semi-finalists, we made our final
selection.

This committee followed a set and somewhat standard procedure, and even included a background check. Nine months after his installation, this senior pastor left the congregation.

There may be a number of reasons why a pastor leaves a particular ministry position. What we can be certain of is that no committee, working for more than a year, nor any candidate, uprooting his family to move to a new place, would call this nine-month stint "a ministry success." Nor is this situation an exception. A 2012 survey of 186 pastors revealed that 56 percent remained in their first call four years or less. Another 250 pastors who qualified to be included in the survey were never actually surveyed—they had already left vocational ministry completely.

The old pastoral search model works on the premises that:

- the committee (or congregation) involved in the formation of the job description (the pastoral profile) has adequate understanding of what is required for the position.
- the committee knows how to evaluate candidates against these criteria.
- candidates who apply have a high degree of self-awareness regarding strengths and struggles.
- only qualified pastors self-select into positions for which they would really fit.
- the congregation differentiates between pastors.

Let's take a look at some of the terminology used in this model.

- *The formation of the job description* means an intentional prioritization of the position's expectations, even to the exclusion of nonessential expectations, and a clear articulation of those expectations.

- *Evaluation of those criteria in the candidate* means having a rubric in place that is capable of establishing objective criteria for assessing the skills, characteristics, qualifications, and experience of candidates. At the same time, the rubric must also have allowable space to at least hear and consider subjective and intuitive perceptions.

- *High degree of self-awareness* refers to an individual's ability to honestly evaluate his or her own strengths and struggles, speaking about strengths without pride and struggles without self-deprecation. Self-awareness includes emotional intelligence, active cognition of emotions, and awareness of perception by others.

- *Self-selection* means that those pastors applying for a position do so at their own instigation, as opposed to being recommended or referred by others.

The old model also makes a couple of other assumptions:

- that there are one or more locations or institutions through which candidates look for new positions, and by posting job descriptions in those locations or with those institutions, the greatest number of most-qualified candidates can be identified.

- that the more applicants there are, the better for the church and committee. In fact, this is absolutely not the case. The church in

Colorado, for example, had no shortage of applicants, and still ended up identifying a pastor who stayed only nine months.

QUESTION:

What are some assumptions you have about the pastoral search process?

III. Reality Meets the "Old World"

REALITY CHECK #1: **The best candidates are *not* looking at job boards.** The best candidates are not regularly looking for new jobs. So, the best candidates will *not* be found by posting a job in some public location. Posting a job publically may get many applications, but they will almost certainly not be the *right* applicants.

This means that many, if not most, candidates surfing job boards are either not content or not thriving in their current ministry contexts. Worse, some of these candidates may be running away from conflict or other difficult situations in which they are participants. These candidates will bring to any new context the emotional dis-ease that troubles their current context, whether it be discontent, fatigue, frustration, or conflict.

REALITY CHECK #2: **The best job descriptions are *not* generated in the vacuum created by the departure of the last pastor.** And yet, more often than not, that is how job descriptions come about. As a result, most pastoral job descriptions are broad and generic in some categories and overly specific in other categories. Committees, churches, and even the exiting pastor do not have all the information necessary to craft the job description for the next candidate. This missing information is what former Secretary of Defense Donald Rumsfeld called "unknown unknowns."

REALITY CHECK #3: There are *not* central locations or institutions where either the best candidates are looking or the best jobs get posted. That is a hierarchical model of information storage and transfer that is largely outdated. That model was popularized in the post-World War II business environment. The technological advances of the early twenty-first century have allowed for the rise of a complex system of information storage and transfer—and in such a complex system, *no one* has all the necessary information for any given situation.

REALITY CHECK #4: Evaluation of candidates must begin *before* the first application is received. Otherwise, committees will generate an evaluation model that accounts only for the information available on and provided by the applicants. This results in the formation of questions that tend to be oriented to technical process and personal practices instead of spiritual maturity expressed in three styles: communication, relationship, and leadership. The evaluation process must be tested before it is applied to the first applicant.

REALITY CHECK #5: Many potential candidates are *not* fully aware of their own strengths and struggles and may not be able to evaluate themselves accurately. Self-awareness is an ability cultivated by the repeated practice of listening to how *other* people perceive us and naming the internal emotional and cognitive responses going on inside us in response. Not everyone can do this well. Committees will need to be aware of this and, where possible, seek input from others who know the candidates well.

QUESTION:

What assumptions do you or your committee have about where and how you will identify your next pastor?

IV. Rethinking the Process: A Different Approach

The model proposed here offers a new approach to the pastoral search process. Whereas the old model took more time at the end of the process, this model takes longer at the beginning. But don't let that discourage you—time well spent at the start of the process will help you reap more benefits in the end. This model is more thorough in its up-front evaluation of your church personality, preferences, and practices, and helps develop a rubric for assessing both internal and external candidates equally. It is adaptable to your particulars, but provides structure for outlining the search process. Step 1 assumes that a search committee has already been formed.

STEP 1
Conduct a Leadership Survey

PURPOSE

The purpose of the leadership survey is to **identify areas of core conviction** among the primary power-holders within the congregation.

These might be leaders in formal positions—like elders; deacons; associate, assistant, or other pastors; and support staff—or might be people with substantial informal power, such as a longstanding matriarch of the church. Regardless of church size, a survey of 12 to 20 key leaders should allow the identification of core commitments that the next pastor should embody. These commitments fit into four categories: theological views, communication preferences, relational tendencies, and leadership style.

- *Theological views* are those distinct theological expressions held by the church. For denominational churches, these views are usually captured in a denominational Book of Order. For non-denominational churches, these views are often represented by congregational bylaws, a constitution, or an Order of Governing. This is usually the easiest of the four categories to define, which explains why many pastoral job descriptions overemphasize it compared to the others.

  QUESTION: *What documents outline the theological preferences of your church?*

- *Communication preferences* are the specific structures of communication preferred in the church. This is not about *where* information is placed, whether in a bulletin or on a website, but specifically *how* information is communicated. Communication style falls into two categories: *chronological-concrete* and *patterned-abstract*. People who prefer the chronological-concrete communication style tend to share information in very specific (five senses) terms. Information is generally presented chronologically and with detail. People who prefer the patterned-abstract approach communication style tend to share information more abstractly. Information tends to be conveyed in generalities, often with the use of metaphors and analogies.

QUESTION: *Using these two categories, how do the majority of people in your church receive and present information?*

- **Relationship tendencies** refer to whether a congregation is primarily *initiating* or *receiving*. People and organizations that practice *receiving* tend to value reflection, internal processing, and quiet. People and organizations that practice *initiating* tend to value talking and external processing. No congregation is exclusively one or the other, but most congregations have as a preferred practice one or the other. How do you know what you are as a congregation? One indicator is how the congregation interacts after the service. In the church where I grew up, the congregation left after worship by way of the front door, shaking hands with the pastor, and was out of the parking lot within five minutes of the service ending. The church was composed largely of internal processors for whom an hour-long service engaging with people and ideas was a mental drain. They preferred to leave the church quietly and reflectively. This church had a preference for receiving. At another church, the congregation usually visits in the foyer for nearly an hour after the service has ended. This church values external process and most members get energized standing around engaging in conversation with one another. Both churches have the same sized congregations and both have relationship preferences, but those preferences are expressed differently.

  QUESTION: *Laying aside what you may prefer, using these categories, what would you say is the primary relationship style of your congregation?*

- **Leadership style** refers to how the church views positions of leadership and the power associated with them. To keep it simple, we place leadership styles into two categories:

▷ *A structured-closed leadership style* is well defined. There is no question about who is responsible for what and in which situations. Structured-closed congregations express consistency in their organizational dynamics. They do not prefer change, but instead hold to tried and true practices and tradition. The structured-closed leadership style tends to hold vision at the top of the organization, with implementation flowing out by decree to the rest of the organization. Some people have described this leadership style as rigid or inflexible.

▷ *Unstructured-open congregations* express variety. They do prefer change, look for opportunities to try something different, and like to be viewed as innovative or creative. An unstructured-open leadership style is harder to define because the unstructured aspects vary from church to church. Some common characteristics include:

+ An openness to input from all members of the congregation into most aspects of the leadership process.
+ A tendency to make final decisions late, thereby being open to last-minute information.
+ The propensity to organize the church around loosely structured policies.
+ The sense that events and programs have been pulled together at the last minute.

Some people have described the unstructured-open leadership style as haphazard and unpredictable.

How do you tell if your congregation is structured-closed or unstructured-open? Think about how it responds to an interruption to a set schedule. Many congregants in one church I attended got anxious the Sunday one of the elders kept missing his cues during the Lord's Supper. He stood before everybody else. He sat before everybody else. He went down the wrong aisle at first. This church practices a structured-closed style of leadership.

Another church I worked with practiced an unstructured-open leadership style. During the Sunday morning announcements, an elder shared a prayer update about a member who had been hospitalized. The information was outdated, as pointed out on the spot by another member, who interrupted the elder and began giving a more thorough and updated report. (The elder was delighted to stand corrected!) However, this member also did not know everything and asked a third person to share what he had learned when visiting the hospital the day before. (I am growing antsy just describing the situation.) When it was all over, four people had taken ten minutes of the morning service to speak into the update on one member. This congregation placed a higher priority on many people getting to speak than on the time constraints of the morning schedule.

> **QUESTION:** *Generally speaking, what leadership style does your congregation practice?*

STRUCTURE

The structure of the leadership survey should **establish definable categories.** We recommend using Dr. Philip Douglass's Church Personality Survey, available online for free at *http://www.douglassandassociates.com/*. Each participant in the survey will need to print his or her results so that they can be collated cumulatively. In most organizations, results tend to cluster into one primary style and one secondary style.

OUTCOME

The outcome of the leadership survey is **a set of practical behaviors and practices** that are common between the primary style of the church and the new senior/solo pastor. In the event that the committee is tasked with hiring a new assistant/associate pastor, the senior/solo pastor should participate in the leadership survey. Usually, a senior/solo pastor will be seeking an assistant/associate who is neither contrasting nor consistent, but complementary in ministry skills, gifts, and passions.

STEP 2
Engage and Establish Committee Dynamics:
A Committee Exercise

PURPOSE

The purpose of the following committee exercise is to **help the committee *own* the process of becoming a non-anxious, unhurried, reflective, and fully engaged group** that can focus on its mission with a minimum of distraction. Outside advisors, consultants, or practitioners can provide helpful insight and advice, but the actual work toward developing into a cohesive group rests with the committee.

The committee exercise can be approached as a day-long retreat or as multiple two-hour meetings stretched over several weeks. We recommend a process that would begin with the retreat and make room throughout the committee's ongoing work to come back and revisit observations from the exercise.

The rationale for such an exercise is this: The leadership survey will provide enough content to generate healthy discussion within the search committee. If a committee allows healthy discussion to continue, differences will emerge between the various members. How a committee responds to these differences expressed by its members will shape the rest of the pastoral search process.

A committee that makes room for differences—even substantial differences that are fervently but respectfully held—has taken the first step toward healthy group dynamics. That committee will ask more honest questions of itself. The members will share more deeply of their own hopes and experiences. They will ask more honest questions of the candidates they evaluate. They will advocate assertively for their views, while being more likely to submit to one another in love (Eph. 5:21). These groups develop a resilience that can stand up to external pressure, usually the pressure to act more quickly. These groups respond to the challenge before them and allow for the process defining their actions to mature (Friedman, 24).

A committee that fears differences from within itself or the broader congregation will react quite differently. This committee will push for homogeneity and insist upon total agreement. Minority views will be ignored, dismissed, or silenced. The dominant perspective will be held uncritically and in the absence of self-reflection. Ambiguity is eliminated through a frenetic pursuit of greater and more precise data that can be used to substantiate the majority opinion.

Committees need to be aware of how people react and respond when faced with significant change. Pastors in transition generally experience 10–15 of the top 50 life stressors as measured by the Life Events Inventory, including starting a new job, changes in responsibility at work, changes to income, serious restriction of social life, the challenge of getting to know new neighbors, and behavior problems in children (Spurgeon, 288).

Congregations experience many of these same stressors. These include but are not limited to:

- The loss of a beloved pastor and his family.
- A period of substantial conflict surrounding the last pastor (or possibly this coupled with the sense of loss listed above).
- Relational pain.
- Financial and organizational uncertainty.
- Anxiety over the future.
- Frustration with unmet expectations.

- Hurt over real or perceived offenses, often involving how and when communication is presented.
- Disappointment in the face of unfulfilled hopes and dreams.
- Concern for their own or others' well-being during the time of transition.

Growing out of this tumultuous period, there is pressure on church leaders and committee members to quickly fill the "leadership void" and get the new pastor in place. This is true whether you are replacing a senior pastor, a youth pastor, or a music minister. Most of us find a sense of personal identity in the spheres of life where our passions and our commitments overlap. When these spheres are disrupted, it creates anxiety. Anxiety is uncomfortable, even painful. And we want the pain to stop.

This anxiety is often behind the pressure that the congregation or church leadership will place upon the search committee, or the pressure the search committee places upon itself. If the committee is not able to mitigate the pressure and remain a non-anxious presence, then the committee will default to a more hurried approach, though still needing to deal with a complicated and rigorous pastoral evaluation process. But no complicated process can account for the complexity of a system in which all people and the system are in flux and changing all along the way.

STRUCTURE

The structure of the committee exercise includes three important phases.

1. Beginning Phase. The beginning phase is intended to **dispel assumptions**. Some of the assumptions inherent in a search committee are that the members know the church well and that they know one another well. Regardless of the degree to which members of a committee know one another, the nature of the work they are undertaking will reveal new insights and unknown aspects of each member. The committee will gain insights into the inside workings of the organization, some of which will be difficult to process. Put simply, when you work on a specific job, in order to accomplish the work, you will have to reveal hidden truths about who you are. Common comments from committees going through this phase include:

- "I never knew that about you."
- "I never would have guessed you had that experience."
- "I am surprised to find that you experienced similar challenges."

In the beginning phase, each committee member should be ready to respond to questions or statements such as:

- Tell a story about a time you experienced real love from the congregation.
- Share a story about a time when you felt connected to other people in our congregation.
- Tell about a time when you felt isolated, alone, or misunderstood in our congregation.
- Talk about your personal experience with a ministry that you are passionate about seeing the church continue under the next pastor.
- Share a story about a time when you connected cognitively or emotionally with the last pastor (that is, the last person who held the position the committee is seeking to fill).

We are generally comfortable sharing broadly what we love or are excited about. Most of us are more likely to share the difficult and challenging times only with people who know us best, people with whom we feel safe. Because of the nature of the job of the committee—to find a pastor for your church—the people on the committee have to become those people with whom you feel *safe*.

This does not mean you share every detail about every struggle you have ever experienced. But it does require a degree of honesty that few of us readily share with a wide group of fellow church members. If a committee has been formed with intentionality, drawing together both men and women of different ages, from various backgrounds, and with different experiences in the church, there are some people on the committee who will not know each other well. These beginning-phase questions are intended to expose the assumptions that all the committee members know one another, love one another, and are completely agreed about every aspect of the church. This simply is not the reality. Two people who never disagree on anything have brokered a false peace, sacrificing their individuality for participation in a shallow collective.

2. The Working Phase. In the working phase, the **questions become more personal** and there are opportunities for self-reflection with more honesty and greater specificity. The committee will want to explore such things as the following:

- Share a story about a time when you were confused about the direction of the church as it pertains to a particular ministry, a specific change, or an aspect of the vision.
- Tell about a time when you were frustrated with something at the church.
- Tell about a disappointment you have experienced at the church.
- Share a story about a time you were saddened by a direction the church went.

How committee members respond to these prompts may even be perceived as a threat to others in the room. One committee I worked with was fairly divided over a visual arts ministry that the church sponsored. In the beginning phase, some members spoke with enthusiasm about the scope of the arts ministry. In the working phase, a different group of members expressed concern that the arts ministry had grown to overshadow other long-standing ministries, some of which had been canceled. This made them sad.

It is important not to dismiss comments like this. The committee must be a safe place for members to speak about their experiences because those experiences are *real*, even though not everyone on the committee will "agree" with them or will have experienced them in the same way. The interpretation of those experiences or events (that is, the assignment of value to them) may be subjective, but the experiences and events themselves were real. Preventing members from sharing their experiences creates a façade that communicates to pastoral candidates that everybody on the committee is unified around a particular vision or ministry, in this case the visual arts ministry. Allowing members to work through the difficulty of graciously and lovingly expressing dissenting views prepares the committee to engage with candidates more honestly.

The key words here are *graciously* and *lovingly*. This is not a time for slander, accusation, or blame. There is no place for "You" statements: This is *your* fault. When you made the decision to cancel the women's tea, I was hurt. Identifying differences within the committee is not the same thing as creating dissention. Personal narratives should be shared with an emphasis on how they were experienced, for example:

- When it was decided that the arts ministry would take priority over the women's tea, I felt confused and sad. In 20 years, I never missed a women's tea, and I did not understand why it was discontinued.

- When I realized that VBS was prioritized over the homeless ministry, I was angry at first. I put a lot of time into developing relationships with people living on the street. I just did not understand the reasons for that decision.

- I remember when they disbanded the Sunday school class I taught. We had a great thing going and suddenly it ended. I was really saddened by the decision. It left me feeling empty and unappreciated. For a long time after, I did not even want to be in a Sunday school class.

Some will observe that there is an acting person or group in each of these situations, and that individual or group was responsible for the change in ministry vision or implementation. This is true, but none of the examples described above are blatant sin. Often, when we experience a difference in opinion, the negative emotions we experience drive us to find a biblical defense that substantiates our perspective and diminishes opposing views.

For example, one committee member I worked with was feeling less valued as the church grew. Unbelievers were coming to know the Lord, but from his perspective it was changing the church. One of the ministries that had suffered during the time of growth was visitation to shut-ins. At a congregational meeting, he publically accused the leaders of failing in their Acts 6 duty to widows and their James 1 duty to orphans. In so doing, he damaged the reputation of the leaders and even drove away some of the newcomers at the church.

If there is unresolved or unconfessed sin between members of the committee, these issues need to be dealt with outside of and away from the work of the committee. The working phase is intended to expose potential sticking points for the committee specifically as each member is a representative of a segment of the church's population.

3. The Ending Phase. In the ending phase, committees should work to **summarize their collective insights** from this exercise. However, the most important outcome of the exercise is not some document or agreed-upon position, but the ability of the committee to work together, with peace and passion, without capitulating to external anxiety or succumbing to internal criticism.

The ending phase will often produce a set of guidelines to which the search committee members voluntarily agree. Here are some examples of guidelines that different committees have come away with and used to guide their search process:

- Our group is mostly extraverted except for Kathy. We realized we just moved along quickly without ever creating a quiet place for her to think and speak. After every five minutes of discussion around a topic, the committee agrees to pause so the chairman can ask Kathy what she is thinking.

- Several of our members, including the chairman, are doers. They want to close discussion and move to action quickly. During the committee exercise, some members were able to share how that made them feel rushed and their views dismissed. We agreed as a committee not to "rush to judgement" in any decision until all the members have had the chance to speak into the matter at hand.

- There is so much talking and so many ideas. We agreed that a secretary would type up the minutes from our meeting and send them to all the committee members. This would keep us on the same page, as well as give us time to process what we had discussed the night before.

- Our last pastor fell into sexual immorality. We wanted to explore that point with future candidates. However, some of the men on the committee didn't want the female committee members in the room when those discussions took place. After a long discussion, we agreed that anybody who wanted to could recuse himself or herself from those discussions. Also, we agreed that the form of the questions asked would be clear, concise, and written down so that they were asked in a very structured way.

OUTCOME

The desired outcome of the committee exercise is to **move the committee toward being the group it should be to function best:** a non-anxious, unhurried, reflective, and fully engaged group that can focus on its mission with a minimum of distraction.

STEP 3

Conduct a Congregational Survey

PURPOSE

The purpose of a congregation survey is to **identify the central commonalities within the church, as well as the differences that exist.** Many church-goers hold to the overly idealistic belief that everyone in the church is "super friendly and all love each other." In reality, there are often extreme differences within congregations. Failing to identify these on the front end predisposes the elected search committee to the goal of unanimity in decision making.

Also, these unnamed differences set the new pastor up for failure. Any changes the new pastor makes will put him at odds with some members of the congregation, even if these are changes the search committee or session board has "endorsed on behalf of the congregation."

One church in the Atlanta area hired a new pastor to replace its founding pastor, who had taken another position in another state. During the candidate evaluation process, the elder board of the church expressed a desire to experiment with the Sunday morning liturgy. The elder board even wanted to get a podium, which the church had never had. The podium was present during the new pastor's first week at the church. Three months into the new pastor's tenure, the church had an informal congregational meeting to see how the church was experiencing the transition. Multiple congregants expressed concern about the "widespread changes" the new pastor was making, one of which was the podium. The elder board had agreed to the change, the search committee had agreed to the change, and the new pastor had agreed to the change, but people in the congregation had not—a fact of which neither the search committee nor the new pastor was aware.

STRUCTURE

The structure of the congregational survey should **prescribe boundaries as well as invite reflection**.

- *Prescribing boundaries* means framing questions and lists in such a way as to exclude "extreme irrelevance." For example, a church that has a high view of Scripture—that the Bible is the inspired Word of God—as a core value, would not ask, "In what ways would you like our church to deemphasize our use of the Bible?"

- *Inviting reflection* means providing enough open-ended questions to get church members thinking about and bringing to the table the best parts of who they are, including gifts and passions. Every member of Christ's body has gifts. Often the structure of an organization limits the opportunities for some people to contribute meaningfully. The loss of a key leader is often the impetus for organizational change, providing members an opportunity to express gifts that have not had an outlet before. As one employee said, "For forty years, I gave all my efforts. If the company had asked, I would have given my heart. They never did."

Supplement 1 at the end of this book is a sample congregational survey. Do not view this list of questions as either authoritative or comprehensive. Rather, the questions are intended to show the variety and focus of questions common to such congregational surveys.

To be clear, this is not an adequate survey for most churches in its present form. It is neither specific enough to your own context, nor focused enough to identify issues important to you. It is intended to be an example of the types of questions and overall structure you may want to ask.

Here are **two important things to keep in mind** as you construct a survey for your church:

- **Avoid what we call the *prioritization of order*.** This is the tendency to put items in the order of their perceived value: first, second, third, etc. One congregational survey took this approach, ordering all lists by the priorities held by the search committee. The first four priorities for the next pastor were (1) preaching, (2) teaching, and (3) leading, all from (4) a Reformed perspective. When the survey was tabulated, these four priorities received the highest individual ratings. However, when the congregation had an honest conversation about deficiencies in the last pastor compared with the core values of the congregation, teaching and leading declined in importance while visitation, fellowship development, and mercy orientation rose higher on the list. The tendency toward prioritization of order is especially true for Western cultures that approach lists from the top to the bottom, and from most important to least important. To avoid prioritization of order, regularly change the order of items in a list from one question to the next. This forces evaluators to engage with items on their own merits instead of by the order in which they are placed.

- **Vary the types and progress of question complexity.**
  Questions start broad and then narrow, and questions move from
  simple (e.g., multiple choice and value rating) to complex (e.g., opinion
  and reflection). The best surveys are instructional as well as inviting,
  and provide insight. For example, a committee might introduce a
  question about preaching like this: *Our last pastor preached on average 80
  times in each of the last five years. When you think of preaching, rate the
  importance of the following components.* The introductory statement
  provides both data and context for the question, which generates
  deeper engagement in the survey participant.

OUTCOME

The outcome of the congregational survey is to **identify and name
actual clusters of congregational unanimity and congregational
variance**: Where is there almost complete agreement within the congregation? What and how are differences expressed in our congregation?

A summary of the survey should be presented to the congregation in
order to make people aware of the areas where they are in agreement and
where there are differences of opinion. Naming the areas of agreement re-
assures the congregation of the basic profile for the next pastor. Naming the
areas of difference reminds the congregation that each pastor is different—
there are not redundancies in the body of Christ—and that the next pastor
will need to lead a congregation that is not unified on every minor point.

The Church Profile

Many search committee members have expressed the view that a church profile is unnecessary for the pastoral search process. To be fair, these members typically believe that their longevity within the church and their familiarity with the history and people of the congregation are sufficient to inform them of the leadership needs within their organization.

The more we work with groups, the more apparent it becomes that people tend to downplay differences. People in positions of formal power or informal influence tend to downplay differences because these differences are not perceived as a threat to their desired goals and outcomes. People motivated to honor core values tend to downplay differences in order to achieve a greater sense of harmony and unity.

Failing to acknowledge and even name differences within a group of people is something the majority culture or majority perspective can afford to do, at least for a season. This can lead to a false sense of homogeneity. By comparison, individuals of the minority culture, perspective, opinion, or belief tend to be acutely aware of the differences within the group. These individuals cannot remain viable, contributing members of the community or group without a constant awareness of the majority culture perspective.

A church profile names these differences among the members of the congregation and identifies these differences among the leaders of the church. It does this in three main ways:

- The church profile **captures the diversity of practices and views within the leadership**, particularly as these differences are expressed in leadership practices, relationship values, and communication styles.

- A robust church profile should **also identify points of continuity and discontinuity** between the organizational expressions of leadership, relationship, and community, and those same expressions dominant in the immediate geographic, ethnic, and cultural contexts of the church.

- Finally, a good church profile will **raise questions that the leaders of the church should seek to answer** as part of the pastoral search process.

A sample Church Profile is available as Supplement 2 at the end of this handbook.

STEP 4
Job Description, Version 1

Your committee now understands the preferences of your church leadership (Leadership Survey) and has identified and named the differences existing within the congregation (Congregational Survey), and your committee
understands the organization as a whole (Church Profile). Your committee
also has a level of differentiated self-awareness (Committee Dynamics Reflection Exercise). All along the way, you have made observations, identified
essential qualities of your next pastor, and perhaps even made a list of
preferences. It is now time to build the pastoral job description.

PURPOSE

The purpose of the job description is to **outline primary responsibilities and goals for the incoming pastor**. The biggest mistake committees make in crafting the job description is to make it either too generic
or too specific.

Overly Generic Job Descriptions. One actual pastoral job description
we received stated in the criteria for the new pastor that he "be a dedicated follower of Jesus Christ, have a heart and passion for God's people, the
church, and have the gift of preaching." This overly generic job description
has the potential of soliciting a large number of interested applicants. In
reality, this only creates more work for the committee, and leaves a number
of unanswered questions:

- *How* does the new pastor show he is a dedicated follower of Jesus Christ?
- What are the *ways* in which the new pastor communicates his passion
  for God's people?
- *How* is the gift of preaching measured or determined?

And the fact remains: every pastor must also either do administration or oversee an administrator. In addition, there are visitation, outreach, teaching, discipleship, mercy, and care, and different congregations value these with different levels of priority. To make an overly generic job description is unfair to the candidates and unhelpful to the search committee.

Overly Specific Job Descriptions. Overly specific job descriptions are problematic to the other extreme. Overly specific job descriptions are usually an attempt to capture everything about a beloved, retiring pastor, or else they are an attempt to manage in unhealthy ways how a new pastor spends his time and where he invests his energy.

A job description that defines every moment of a pastor's time and describes every aspect of his ministry does not account for the fact that every pastor is unique. There is no redundancy in the body of Christ. There is not a younger version of your best-loved pastor somewhere out there. You cannot prevent getting another pastor who struggles with the same sins simply by asking enough detailed questions. Overly specific job descriptions do not account for the unique personality and gifts of the next person you will call to be your pastor.

You want the next person to bring the best of who he is to the role of pastor—all of his gifts (Ephesians 4) and all of his skill, experiences, and capacities. Overly specific job descriptions will also solicit a number of applicants. Some of these people will attempt to change the job description through interaction with the committee. Others will attempt to fill every aspect of the job description, usually with tragic results to their own health, ministry, marriage, family, and the church.

STRUCTURE

An effective job description that **captures all the essential qualities needed without being overly generic or overly specific** will usually contain these elements and be structured along these lines:

- Core values (theological and corporate)
- Gifting (spiritual, physical, mental, relational)
- Capacity (leadership, administrative, etc.)
- Experience (vocationally and in other areas)

A sample senior pastor job description can be found in Supplement 1 at the end of this handbook.

OUTCOME

The outcome here is **to produce a document that captures the essential components** growing out of the information captured from the surveys of the leadership and the church. This is the *first draft* of your job description, which implies that, at some point, there will be a second draft, and there is. But this is not something you, your committee, your leaders, your church, or your last pastor can provide. You need "experts."

STEP 5

Input From "Best-Fit Candidates"

Best-fit candidates are **individuals who meet the criteria for the first-draft job description, but who are not seeking a new position**. Instead, best-fit candidates are faithfully serving where God has placed them. They are experts in their own experience with organizations of similar sizes and dynamics.

- **Best-fit candidates** are actual serving pastors that you as a committee contact.

- **Meeting the criteria for the job description** means pastors who have 48–60 months of experience in a position similar to the one you are seeking to fill. Is your committee looking for a senior pastor for your church of 300 people? Best-fit candidates are senior pastors of churches with 300 (or more) people. Are you in a suburban church with 180 members looking for an assistant pastor? Best-fit candidates are assistant pastors with five years' experience and currently serving in a similar context.

  The committee should find people currently serving in similar contexts because these pastors have first-hand knowledge of a similar church setting, giving them the ability to observe, state concerns, and ask questions about your first-draft job description.

  It is also important to start with candidates who are not looking to leave their current positions. In our experience, candidates who are looking to leave their current positions bring with them a level of frustration and discontent, often involving conflict of some kind. Later in the process there will be a time to look at candidates who are seeking to leave their current positions, as well as candidates who self-select into the application pool. But at this point, when a search committee is in the beginning phases of developing "muscle memory" around a process that is, for the most part, entirely new, it is challenging to examine a candidate who is not able to bring to the table only the best of who he or she is.

- **Faithfully serving where God has placed them** means that there is every indication that the best-fit candidate is active, productive, and effective in his or her current ministry position.

- *Experts in their own experience* means that these people have gained relevant experience in situations pertinent to your leadership needs. These people have navigated those experiences with enough regularity that they have developed best practices applicable in similar situations—and can express their experience with personal and situational specificity, providing helpful reflection on the process.

PURPOSE

The purpose of interviewing best-fit candidates is to **get real, present-day input on the quality of your first-draft job description, from actual pastors**. Ideally, you will identify four or five best-fit candidates.

STRUCTURE

The committee's interaction with the best-fit candidates begins by **asking them to donate an hour of their time first to evaluate and then to talk through with the committee their observations and perceptions of the first-draft job description**. You want to know from best-fit candidates what their concerns are. What are the holes in the description? What is unrealistic or overly optimistic? What is exciting about the position? What would cause them to hesitate to apply for your or a similar position? It is invaluable to have someone qualified for and skilled in the type of position you are trying to fill tell you exactly why he would or would not consider your position.

One search committee asked a best-fit candidate, a pastor in another city, to evaluate their first-draft job description. After a long hour of back-and-forth, the pastor bluntly stated, "I would never take this job. There is no way one person could complete half of these goals at a church of your size working 80 hours a week." The committee thanked the best-fit candidate for his perspective, but they did not change the job description. The pastor they eventually hired to the position left both the position and the ministry because of burnout after less than two years.

OUTCOME

The outcome from interaction with the best-fit candidates is to **collect and compile the feedback**. The committee should then work to adjust the job description based on the feedback from these candidates.

The easier part is to incorporate the feedback in order to generate the second-draft job description. The harder part may be to change your expectations as a committee or the expectations of the congregation and leadership. The first-draft job description will reflect the hopes and desires, as well as the values, of your congregation. To make the job description more realistic, based on feedback from actual pastors doing the same type of work, means having to disappoint people. A member who expects the pastor to visit every congregant and a member who wants the pastor to spend 25 hours a week on sermon preparation will not both be happy with the same pastor. One of them will be sorely disappointed or, more likely, they will both experience varying degrees of disappointment.

Adjusting and editing the job description can open up new layers of stress or disappointment, as committee members concede unrealistic or simply unattainable expectations and outcomes for the next pastor. We recommend that, whenever new points of stress, anxiety, frustration, disappointment, or hurt are exposed, the committee revisit the committee exercise section, dedicating time to processing these emotional realities together.

Part of the job of a search committee is to bring unrealistic expectations for the next pastor back into line with reality. John Ortberg put it this way: "Leadership is the art of disappointing people at a rate they can stand." This is going to cause people stress. They will get frustrated. They will hold onto the belief that there is a better pastor out there. This is perhaps the hardest part of the search committee's work, but it is work for which the committee is prepared if they have developed strong relationships and differentiation.

STEP 6
Job Description, Version 2

PURPOSE

The purpose of the second draft of the job description is to **refine the description based on the input from the best-fit candidates you talked with**. No doubt you will need to make many changes to what you had in the first draft.

The committee should determine to what degree the feedback from best-fit candidates is incorporated into the job description. A committee might overlook such feedback when it pertains to secondary concerns or minor objections. But a committee that fails to make adjustments based on concerns of substance expressed by multiple best-fit candidates is setting its next pastor up for failure.

One committee summarized the expectations for the next pastor like this: "We are looking for a younger version of Rev. Smith." Numerous best-fit candidates expressed concern over this statement. One said, "I have a lot of the philosophical approaches and theological commitments of Rev. Smith. I think I even have a similar preaching style and approach. But I know I approach congregational care very differently. Your description does not account for the uniqueness of who I am and the different experiences I bring to the position."

The committee dismissed the concerns expressed by these best-fit candidates. Ultimately, it extended a call to a pastor who said he would seek to be a younger version of their retiring, long-term pastor. Within a year of taking the position, the church had declined in membership from 120 to 30 members, with a weekly attendance of only 25.

STRUCTURE

Based on the input received and the level of incorporation of that input the committee decides upon, **the second draft of the job description can be prepared, following a structure similar to the first but with improvements and refinements where necessary**.

OUTCOME

Once you have a refined job description that better fits your position, the committee is ready to begin interacting with actual candidates.

STEP 7
Identifying a Pool of Actual Candidates

PURPOSE

After revising the job description, the committee will want to **begin identifying a list of actual candidates who fit the job criteria and whom the group would like to pursue further**.

A committee may want to go back to one of the best-fit candidate who provided input on the job description and ask, "Will you put *your* name in for the position?" Remember, best-fit candidates are individuals who meet the criteria for the first-draft job description, but are not seeking a new position because they are faithfully serving where God has placed them. But these are experts in their own experience with organizations of similar sizes and dynamics. Nothing in this description prevents a committee from asking best-fit candidates to be actual candidates. One church in Nashville contacted several best-fit candidates for an assistant pastor position. After a lengthy interaction with the first person, the committee asked him to put his name in for the position. He declined, but the committee members were so convinced he was their candidate that they asked the senior pastor to call the candidate. After two hours of talking with the senior pastor—during which the candidate came to better understand the senior pastor's vision for the position—he applied, was accepted, and became the next assistant pastor.

STRUCTURE

Whether or not best-fit candidates are willing to consider the position, committees should ask best-fit candidates for recommendations. Best-fit candidates are the ideal people to make such recommendations. Committees should specify what qualities or traits in the best-fit candidates they are looking for in those recommended for the position:

- "We really appreciated your articulation of the gospel. Can you recommend other candidates who would have similar theological commitments and gospel articulation?"

- "Your approach to congregational care resonated with us. We really sensed your compassion for suffering people. Can you recommend other people with a similar passion?"

This is one place a committee can over-extend itself. Ideally, a committee is working with 5 to 8 candidates at a time, and rarely more than 13 at a time. The more candidates a committee is attempting to evaluation at one time, the less thorough their evaluation tends to be.

In identifying a pool of actual candidates, we recommend employing the **referral method**. By not posting your job in a public place, like an online job board, you avoid the potential flood of self-selecting candidates.

- Begin the process by asking **best-fit candidates** for recommendations.
- Then consider other recommendations from **people who know your church**.
- Finally, consider recommendations made by **people in your broader church networks**, presbyteries, or denominational agencies, who know the candidates they are recommending.

Only *after* building a strong pool of viable candidates through the referral process should a committee even consider posting the job in a public place. Even then, we recommend having it posted no longer than a month, ideally only two weeks. The diagram below gives a visual representation of what this process looks like.

KNOW THE CHURCH / KNOW THE CANDIDATE	DON'T KNOW THE CHURCH / KNOW THE CANDIDATE
IDEAL CANDIDATES	*RECOMMENDATIONS BY OTHERS*
RECOMMENDATIONS BY PASTORS OR PEOPLE IN THE CHURCH	*JOB BOARD APPLICANTS*
KNOW THE CHURCH / DON'T KNOW THE CANDIDATE	DON'T KNOW THE CHURCH / DON'T KNOW THE CANDIDATE

OUTCOME

At this point, your committee should be functioning as a cohesive yet diverse group, you will have established the processes and procedures you will use, and **defined a set of potential candidates within which you will seek the one to fill your open position**. The most challenging part of your work is just beginning.

PART TWO

The Candidate Evaluation Process

I. The Interview Process

PURPOSE

The purpose of the interview process is, of course, to **give the committee and the candidates an opportunity to get to know each other, ask questions of each other, and move toward committee consensus on which candidate(s) to pursue further**.

STRUCTURE

Throughout the interviewing process, we recommend use of the **behavioral interviewing approach**. This is also referred to as the **STAR approach**. STAR is an acronym for **Situation or Task, Action, and Results**. We have adjusted the STAR approach to fit more precisely the non-profit and ministry context, as outlined in the chart below.

S.S.T.A.R.R. Interviewing

S SET THE STAGE	Questions have contexts. By giving some context to the candidate, you set him/her up for answering most honestly. Acontextual questions can feel like a trap or "set-up".
S SITUATION OR **T** TASK	Ask the candidate to describe a situation where the skills, competencies, or expressions of character are likely to be revealed. This description should be very specific about the details, who was involved and what their relationships were, and what the goals and objectives were. The situation may be from a past ministry position, other employment, volunteer, or other relevant context.
A ACTION (YOU TOOK)	Ask the candidate to describe what actions or steps he/she took in order to reach the objectives or address the issue. Encourage a detailed accounting of the process.
R RESULTS (YOU ACHIEVED)	What were the outcomes? What happened? What were the results? What was accomplished?
R REFLECTION	What did the candidate learn? How might he/she approach a similar situation differently as a result of this experience?

A few comments about the addition of the **Setting the Stage** and the **Reflection** elements are in order. First, differentiated committees will ask questions about the spiritual nature, ethical behavior, and sinful tendencies of candidates they are evaluating. As indicated before, the committee will only ask those questions if they approach the committee exercise with a commitment to learning and growth. Even so, such questions can be startling or off-putting to candidates. By setting the stage, committees provide context to candidates, reassuring them, and increasing the likelihood of getting mature, well-considered responses from candidates.

Consider questions like these:

- How do you address and resolve conflict?
- When is the last time you looked at pornography?
- What does it mean to be a leader?

These questions are direct and border on confrontational, and they provide no context for why they are being asked. The candidate on the receiving end has very little experience with your committee and your church. This leaves the candidate to speculate on how safe it is to respond honestly.

One church asked a candidate, "When is the last time you looked at pornography?" The candidate was honest about when it was, and went on to explain the steps he took to pursue support of other Christians and, over time, sobriety in this area. However, one committee member had watched her son-in-law destroy her daughter's marriage through addiction to pornography. She reacted negatively to the candidate's response and said they should never consider hiring a pastor who had ever viewed pornography. The committee was split on how to proceed. Eventually, the members decided not to move forward with that candidate. However, they also removed that question from the interview process. The anxiety of one committee member resulted in removing a question that provided the committee with important insights.

Committees do need to ask hard questions of candidates, even questions related to sexuality and conflict—but they need to ask those questions within a setting-the-stage framework that provides context and self-awareness that give helpful direction to the candidate for framing his or her responses. Now, consider these reworded versions of the above questions using the SSTARR method. The steps are broken out using the following abbreviations:

- Setting the Stage (S1)
- Situation (S2) or Task (T), or Situation and Task together (ST)
- Action (A)
- Results (R1)
- Reflection (R2)

SAMPLE BEHAVIORAL INTERVIEWING QUESTIONS:

- (S1) Any time you get two people together, there is the potential for conflict. We as a committee have seen that even as we work through this process. (ST) Tell us about a time when you experienced conflict with someone (not in your family). What was the situation? (A) How did you respond? (R1) What was the outcome? What did you learn? (R2) Looking back, how have you reflected on that situation?

- (S) We live in a highly sexualized culture. Nobody has escaped it unaffected. (S1) Tell us about a time you experienced sexual temptation. (A) What steps did you take to pursue purity and sobriety in the face of that temptation? (R1) How did those steps help deliver you from the temptation? (R2) As you reflect back on that temptation, what would you do the same/differently? How would you counsel and minister to someone experiencing a similar temptation?

- (S1) Leadership is a term that is used a great deal, but can have very different meanings depending on who you ask. We recognize different kinds of leadership at work on our search committee. (S2) Tell us about a time you engaged in the task of leadership, where there was disagreement, in order to accomplish a specific result. What was the situation? (A) What steps/actions did you take? What was the response? How did you work toward mutual submission? (R1) What was the final outcome/result? (R2) What did you learn from that experience?

A longer list of sample behavioral interviewing questions is found in Supplement 2, at the end of this handbook.

What should be obvious is that it takes a great deal more energy, attention, and care to formulate behavioral interviewing questions. They also take more time to ask and to answer. This is why we recommend a **combination of both written and verbal behavioral interviewing questions**.

One other note: questions should not be simply biographical, technical, or speculative. Here are samples of those types of questions:

- **Biographical:** Tell us about your family.
- **Technical:** How do you go about preparing your sermon?
- **Speculative:** How would you help our church grow in being more evangelistic?

A committee will receive a ministry form or pastoral resume, which provides background and insight into biographical questions. Technical questions can be asked if they are deemed essential, but they rarely are at this stage in the process. Speculative questions will only solicit speculative responses, loosely based on experience, and lacking the contextual information necessary to provide an accurate response.

WRITTEN QUESTIONS. The **purpose** of written questions is to **honor the gifting of unique candidates**, some of whom will communicate best in writing, while others will communicate best in speaking.

The **structure** of the written questionnaire should **include five well-developed questions that grow out of the information gathered in your previous committee work and should follow the SSTARR rubric.** These questions should be relevant to all candidates who are applying for the position, whether they are internal candidates or external candidates. Five well-developed questions should take candidates about an hour to answer in detail. This is enough of a time commitment that people not really interested in the position will not bother completing the questionnaire, but not so large a time commitment that interested candidates cannot find time to complete it.

The **outcome** of the written questions is **a baseline against which all candidates are evaluated** on issues central to the church, the culture, and the current ministry position.

After reviewing a candidate's responses to the written questions and before arranging a verbal interview, committee members should listen to at least two of that candidate's sermons, lectures, or presentations. This provides specific insight into the candidate's approach to ministry, aspects that can be further explored in the verbal interview.

VERBAL QUESTIONS. Based on how each candidate answers the written behavioral questions, and taking into consideration information provided on resumes or ministry forms, search committees should formulate a second round of questions, but where the written questions were uniform across all candidates, these verbal questions may vary from one candidate to the next.

The **purpose** of conducting a verbal interview is to **provide insight into specific ministerial aspects:** How have the last five years of ministry been formative in the spiritual and personal aspects of the candidate's life? How does the candidate demonstrate a commitment to active learning? Additionally, the verbal interview **provides insight into more subjective aspects of candidate evaluation:** Does the candidate have an accent that would cause her to stand out in your community? Is he articulate in such a way as to support effectiveness in your area? Can she answer questions about difficult issues with grace and wisdom? Does he speak more decisively or with a sense of unsettled openness?

The **structure** of the verbal questions **may change based on whether the interview is by phone, video, or face-to-face**. However, the questions should still follow the SSTARR rubric.

OUTCOME

The **outcome** of the interview phase is to **further narrow down the field of prospective candidates** to those few that most strongly fit the criteria and show the most promise for filling the position.

II. Engaging with References

PURPOSE

The purpose of engaging with a candidate's references is, hopefully, **to gather more understanding of the character and abilities of the candidate.** Unfortunately, experience reveals that references often provide little or no actual insight into a candidate. There are two common reasons for this.

First, some references fear misrepresenting the candidate and so they share only positive and/or neutral experiences.

Second, some references simply want the candidate to get a job—whether or not that job may be the best fit for him or her. For example, within a few months of taking a new position, one pastor almost split the church with conflict. When one of the elders called the pastor's previous church and asked about that congregation's experience with the issue, a leader honestly confessed, "Yes, we had that issue. We hoped he would do better somewhere else. More than that, we just wanted him to go away."

STRUCTURE AND OUTCOME

Using **behavioral interviewing questions** with references, as well as with a candidate, can improve the results of these interactions. The Setting the Stage phase with references may look a little different than it does with candidates. Your objective in interviewing references is to broaden your perspective as a committee. Communicating that goal with references is likely to get them out of the "strengths/struggles" expectation many have when called to give a reference. You want to understand the perspective of the reference. You want that person to know you value his or her point of view. The goal is not to pit the reference's perspective in tension against what others have said. But, other bits of information can be helpful in providing greater insight.

INSTEAD OF ASKING:	TRY ASKING:
What is one area where this candidate could improve?	As you think about other people in the church, what are some of the concerns you've heard expressed, particularly in areas where the candidate could improve?
How would you rate this candidate's relational skills?	The candidate told us about when a key elder died. Please share with us what you witnessed and how you experienced this candidate during that time.
What is this candidate's greatest strength?	The candidate told us one of his greatest strengths was his preaching. As you think about his preaching, how have you seen him grow in his time at your church?
How does this candidate deal with conflict?	Disappointment often leads to conflict. As you've watched the candidate minister, tell us about a time you saw her deal with people as they wrestled with their disappointment.
Tell us about your experience with the candidate.	The candidate told us about a time when [X] happened. Could you share your observations of that season in the life of the candidate/congregation?

When to Evaluate and Vote on Internal Candidates

Ruling on internal candidates is one of the most challenging aspects of any pastoral search process. *Internal candidates* are people already on staff at your church in one role while a search process is being conducted to fill a second role. Not all qualified and existing staff are internal candidates. To be an internal candidate, the staff member must desire and consent to be considered for the open position.

Internal candidates are people you know. They already serve in your church in another capacity. You watch them minister. You sit under their teaching. You observe their leadership. You talk with them. You have a relationship with them. You already have an opinion about whether this internal candidate could fill or not fill the open pastoral position.

External candidates are people you do not know—at least, not usually—and even if you do, you usually do not know them well. You may have heard about them. Others have shared their insights about these candidates. You have impressions about them. You may anticipate an external candidate's qualifications and capacity to fill the open position.

Committees are willing to engage external candidates in deliberate, informed, robust, and time-heavy ways. That is, more or less, what the pastoral search process is. Unfortunately, many search committees do not believe it is necessary to dedicate the same deliberate, informed, robust, and time-committed approach to internal candidates. The justification is, "We don't need to interview him. We already know enough about him."

By not applying the same sound evaluation approach developed for the search process to internal candidates, search committees set themselves, their congregations, and internal candidates up for party lobbying, relational breakdown, personal frustration, and potentially church-wide conflict. Within every church we have worked with, some church leaders and members love and value the ministry contribution of the internal candidate. These church members would like to see, and often work toward, the internal candidate being promoted. Meanwhile, in the same congregation, there are church leaders and members who are openly opposed to the internal candidate being hired for the position. The following chart graphs these two realities, as constructed from conversations with search committees as they spoke about internal and external candidates:

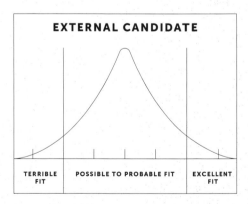
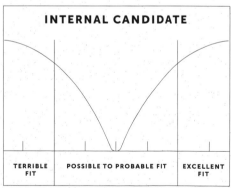

The first chart reveals the assumption that search committees expect most external candidates to fall into the unknown category of "possible/probable fit." A few will be an excellent fit. A few will be a terrible fit. The second chart reveals the assumption that search committees expect their internal candidate to be either an excellent fit or a terrible fit, but rarely if ever in the middle. And if the committee is a fair representation of the congregation, one should expect the congregation to be equally divided on the internal candidate.

The time to evaluate an internal candidate is after the formal search process has been developed and the process has been tested against best-fit candidates. Treat an internal candidate as you would an external candidate. Provide him the same opportunity to answer the behavioral interviewing questions. We even recommend that the committee set aside a "visit" weekend for the internal candidate, to be filled with all the same types of gatherings, meetings, and opportunities for engagement as would be employed during the visit of an external candidate. This gives integrity to the search process. Can it be awkward? Potentially, but if it is done well, it should feel like a fully formed and functioning evaluative process. One way to overcome the awkwardness is to name what you are doing: "The committee wants to look at you with the same thorough, robust evaluation process that we are applying to all our candidates."

Committees often fear ruling on an internal candidate too early in the process. This is understandable. If your assistant pastor wants the senior pastor position and the committee decides not to recommended him for the position, the assistant pastor knows his time in the church is limited. He may leave before a new senior pastor is hired, further straining the ministerial resources within the staff. However, if the committee demonstrates that it has developed a sound evaluative process and employed it equally among all applicants, then the internal candidate (and those rallying for him or her) may still be disappointed, but is less likely to be resentful, even toxic, to the congregation during the transition process.

After the committee has fully evaluated the internal candidate, it needs to rule on whether or not the candidate will receive the recommendation of the committee. *This needs to happen before moving along in the pro-*

cess with external candidates. The decision of the committee should be clearly communicated to the internal candidate with love and truth. This information will need to be carefully conveyed back to the congregation. Often committees will invite the internal candidate into helping develop a process for announcing this decision. This process is painful. There is disappointment. But the character of both the committee and the internal candidate will be revealed in how they mutually handle the decision and subsequent announcement.

Another reason this should be done prior to engaging external candidates is because external candidates will want to know if there is an internal candidate. External candidates regularly decline being considered for a position, even if that person may be the best candidate, until the internal candidate is ruled upon. No external candidate envies a situation where he is being evaluated even as the congregation is waiting to hear whether the internal candidate is being considered. It sets the external candidate up to being "the guy" that drove away the assistant pastor. *Rule on the internal candidate before actively considering external candidates.* If a committee feels unable to make that decision, find more best-fit candidates from whom to seek input.

III. *The Evaluation Process*

At this point, committees employ a variety of actions aimed at establishing further evaluation of a candidate. Some committees schedule a second phone interview with strong candidates. Other committees will go out and observe the candidate in his or her context. There is no one way to engage with candidates in the time between the first verbal interview and a public visit to your church.

PARALLEL CANDIDATE EVALUATION

As long as a committee is willing to receive the application of a new candidate, the committee should approach each candidate in a parallel manner. Here we are using an illustration from electrical circuitry. The two most common structures of an electrical circuit are *series* and *parallel*. When components are in parallel, they are connected so that the same voltage is applied to each component at the same time, without exclusivity.

Committees should feel comfortable having different candidates at any of the previous phases of the process, until the committee is ready to close the application process to new candidates. This means one candidate may just be applying while another candidate has already had two phone interviews. This is the "parallel" aspect of the process.

SERIES CANDIDATE EVALUATION

Once a committee closes the process to new candidates and narrows the pool of candidates down to a select few, the committee has entered the "series" process. In the series process, the committee ranks the final candidates. If there are more than five final candidates, the committee has more work to do in differentiating the candidates from one another. This may include further phone interviews or conversations with a candidate's references.

The Church Visit. Once the candidates are ranked, the next step is to invite the top candidate for a public visit to the church. This visit should include both structured time to meet with key leaders and influence holders within the church, but should also include unstructured time to allow the candidate to drive around the community, pray, and "experience" the area. Usually, the visit will include some kind of formal presentation to the congregation. A pastoral candidate will usually be asked to preach. A youth or women's ministry candidate may be asked to teach a Sunday school lesson or give a presentation.

After the candidate has left, the people responsible for extending the job offer (call)—whether that is the session, the search committee, or the congregation as a whole—should have a yes-or-no vote.

There is not much to say about a yes vote, except perhaps, "Congratulations!" But a no vote should be followed up with something substantial. You are saying no to someone who has committed a substantial amount of time, energy, and prayer into this process with you. Telling a candidate no should be done by phone, and should begin with affirmation of his or her strengths. Be prepared to give a specific reason why the committee, session, or congregation did not extend the job offer. And end the time with an affirmation of the candidate, how the Lord has uniquely made him or her, and how you see the Lord working in his or her life. We encourage you to end that conversation with a time of prayer for the candidate and his or her family.

Perhaps one of the least helpful ways a committee can turn down a candidate at this stage in the process is to say something like, "We've decided to go in a different direction." Such generic statements take away the committee's ability to affirm the candidate's strengths in an honest way.

What a committee should never do is parade a series of top candidates in front of the church and then ask the church to select their favorite. When the committee has followed a thorough process, only the committee members understand all the steps, have all the information, and know all the factors involved in recommending one candidate over another. In situations where the committee only has the power to recommend a candidate, as opposed to actually extending a job offer to that candidate, a church or elder board making the final decision would give great disservice not to strongly consider the candidate the committee recommends. Stated more pointedly, *the group that is finally empowered to make the final decision must be able to state specific reasons justifying the dismissal of a committee recommendation.* Those reasons do exist and regularly so. But they need to be stated clearly.

The problem with presenting the congregation with a series of candidates is the organizational equivalent of the "nipple confusion" that often results when new-born, breast-fed babies are offered a bottle too soon—the infant becomes confused and will not latch on appropriately to *any* source of nutrients. This can cause a lot of pain and discomfort for a mother and potential health issues for the infant.

A committee that presents a series of candidates to a congregation invites dissent. One person or group may latch on to one candidate, while other people or groups will latch on to other candidates. These people or groups do so based on initial impressions and short interactions, but without the knowledge and insight of the thorough assessment process implemented by the search committee. And the candidate who is eventually hired is subject to comparison with other candidates. A candidate who was hired after such a process began hearing from some people in the congregation, "Well, you weren't my first choice anyway."

More About Site Visits. A committee may want a candidate to visit the church "under the radar" as the final, non-public stage of the series evaluation. Often a committee attempts to fill a site visit with as many meetings, gatherings, or interactions as possible. One candidate had two 15-hour days of meetings with individuals and groups, totaling more than 100 people, during his site visit. Very few people have the energy, stamina, and mental fortitude for such a full agenda.

The **purpose** of a site visit is **to give the committee and/or key leaders the opportunity to interact with and observe the candidate, and vice versa**. Meetings should be limited to the individuals (e.g., a senior pastor, if hiring support staff) and groups (e.g., a session or elder board) of most importance, as the final step in candidate evaluation.

The **structure** of a site visit should include **dedicated time with the search committee, time with the staff, and time for the candidate (and family, if applicable) to experience the area**. Dedicated time with the search committee provides a final opportunity for both sides to ask questions, explore possibilities, and discuss the future. Dedicated time with the staff provides both parties the opportunity to test compatibility. Even if there are legitimate reasons the candidate should not meet with all the staff, or even all the full-time staff, he or she should have least have dedicated time with the person to whom he/she will report or supervise.

Finally, it is important to provide the candidate the opportunity to experience the area where the church is located. People need concrete information to inform the decision-making process. What is this area like? How far away do most people live from the church? Where is the nearest grocery store or Wal-Mart? Are there family and pediatric doctors proximate to the area? How long does it take to get from one place to another? Place is important. The love of or attraction to a place, a geography, or a region is not enough to commend a position to a candidate. But if there is not an appreciation for the actual place, ministry to actual people is challenged.

The **outcome** of the site visit will be the **congregational vote on this particular candidate**. If the search committee has done its job well, the candidate will be a good fit with the position and the church, and barring any strong congregational dissent, the appropriate church body will extend a job offer to the candidate. Ideally, the process will conclude with the new person stepping in for a long and fruitful ministry with the congregation.

IV. Ending the Work of the Committee

PURPOSE

Committee members experience a variety of emotions as the process comes to an end. **Ending well is as important as beginning well.**

The search committee is the group of people the new pastor knows best, if only because of the level and frequency of interaction with them. For the committee to simply dissolve immediately upon the arrival of the new pastor can leave the pastor feeling alone in his efforts to navigate his new context. We recommend that there be **some kind of transition committee that takes responsibility for helping the new pastor and family get oriented to the church.** This does not necessarily have to be the search committee, but transition committees work best when members of the search committee are on it, for the sake of continuity.

STRUCTURE AND OUTCOME

As the search committee prepares to dissolve, there should be at least one meeting, if not two, to allow committee members to reflect back over the entire process. This is intended to be a time when committee members can voice the impact of the process on each of their lives. When a committee has meshed well at the beginning, ending can evoke a diversity of emotion: joy at completing the work, sorrow at disbanding, loneliness at the fear that one may not have a voice in the larger church, gratitude for the support of the group, and so on.

Moving from a place of relative importance back into the pew as a fellow church member leaves many committee members feeling sad. If the reason for this sadness is not named—"I have moved from a place of obvious influence into a place of common interaction"—sadness can become fear, even doubt. Members may ask: Why do I feel this way if we hired the right person? Left to their own mental processes, some of the most supportive committee members can become the greatest critics of the new pastor. Having a time of mutual, shared processing as a means of both celebrating and grieving the end of the committee, can provide both the space to name distressing emotions and the context to begin working through those emotions.

This "closing out" meeting is not intended to be a time for committee members to voice their disapproval of the final selection. Those concerns should already have been raised and addressed during the candidate evaluation process.

The search committee should also debrief their closing process with the church leadership, but that should take place at a different meeting. The ending meeting is intended to provide closure while maintaining established confidentiality within the group.

Wise leadership will consider and choose the best way to publically honor the work of the committee, but this should not replace a time for the committee to begin the process of emotional and relational closure to the search process.

Sample Congregational Survey

A. When you think about a pastor, what characteristics come to mind?

B. Even if you have already listed them above, which of the following do you associate with the persona and position of a pastor (check each box that applies)?

	Administration / Organizing		Preaching
	Connecting to Local Community		Relationally Oriented
	Counseling		Rich Prayer Life
	Leadership / Vision		Teaching
	Missions Support		Shepherding

C. Rate in order of importance the following criteria for a pastor, based on your perspective.

	Administration / Organizing
	Connecting to Local Community
	Counseling
	Leadership / Vision
	Missions Support
	Preaching
	Relationally Oriented
	Rich Prayer Life
	Teaching
	Shepherding

D. Rate the following job responsibilities, with 5 being **very important** and 1 being **beneficial but not critical** (please circle your response):

LEADERSHIP / VISION FOR THE FUTURE

Guides spiritual development of staff and lay leadership	1	2	3	4	5
Effectively supervises / coordinates all work of church staff	1	2	3	4	5
Proven leadership skills in managing an organization / staff	1	2	3	4	5
Has a vision for future growth and experience with how to achieve it	1	2	3	4	5

PREACHING

Prepares and delivers compelling sermons based directly on biblical text and doctrinal principles	1	2	3	4	5
Preaching that calls the congregation to a personal faith in Christ, to repentance, spiritual growth, service, and evangelism	1	2	3	4	5
Spends quality time in study of the Word and prayer	1	2	3	4	5
Develops a rich worship life within the church, encouraging the congregation through meaningful connection and blessing in worship experience	1	2	3	4	5
Gospel-centered, life-practical application	1	2	3	4	5

RELATIONALLY ORIENTED / COMMUNITY OUTREACH

Works well in team settings with elected church leaders	1	2	3	4	5
Ability to relate well to people "of a certain age"	1	2	3	4	5
Young in outlook; can relate to younger families with children	1	2	3	4	5
Encourages social outreach through partnerships with the local community	1	2	3	4	5
Strong support for local and worldwide missions activities	1	2	3	4	5

SHEPHERDING / CARE

Promotes a church culture that embodies Christ's example of servant leadership	1	2	3	4	5
Counsels families and individuals of the church	1	2	3	4	5
Visits the sick, shut-ins, hospitals, and potentially new members	1	2	3	4	5
Works with others to promote pastoral care and shepherding	1	2	3	4	5

TEACHING

Is a strong teacher of the Word as well as a preacher	1	2	3	4	5
Proven leadership skills in developing a deep faith commitment/discipleship	1	2	3	4	5
Is an effective and engaging communicator in small group settings	1	2	3	4	5
Develops a rich worship life within the church, encouraging the congregation through meaningful connection and blessing in worship experience	1	2	3	4	5
Emphasizes involvement in Christian education (e.g., Sunday school)	1	2	3	4	5

E. What age do you think our next pastor should be in order to best connect with our congregation?

	30–45		45–55		55–65		no preference

F. Please identify the top five attributes (in order of importance) for our new pastor:

	Agent for change		Intellectually challenging
	Relates to a wide variety of people		Outstanding teacher
	Compassionate		Personable/outgoing
	Experienced in his role		Sociable/comfortable to be with
	Great speaker		Strong leader
	Good Listener		Visionary
	Handles conflict effectively		Welcomes new approaches

G. In a short paragraph, how would you describe our new pastor in your own words to a friend?

Sample Church Personality Report

Prepared for **First Church Sample**
September 28, 2015

INTRODUCTION[1]

We should assume that all churches are unique in the ways they conduct ministry even though they may have similar purposes. The reality is that the culture differs remarkably from one church or organization to another. How an organization is structured, how information is communicated, how implementation is managed, and how people relate are all part of what makes up culture. Culture is your church's personality; it is the DNA of your church's body that makes it think and act like it does.

We know that churches differ in their size, structure, and goals, but they also differ in ministry style. These differences provide insight into the reasons your church behaves as it does in its efforts to serve the Lord of the church. In addition, your church personality points to your most productive ministry path as you engage in your mission.

This report applies the results of the survey taken by leaders and staff members of **First Church Sample** to:

- Identify the church's strengths as well as its challenges.
- Maximize the benefits that arise from the diversity of the church members.
- Minimize the potential problem areas and sources of conflict.
- Develop descriptions to assist in the search for a pastor with a ministry style similar to that of First Church Sample.

Specifically, in light of your particular church culture this Church Personality Report describes the ministry style of the church in the areas of:

1. Communication Style
2. Relationship Style
3. Conducting Out-Reach (In-Reach?)
4. Making decisions,
5. Planning.

For greater detail, refer to the book *What is Your Church's Personality: Discovering and Developing the Ministry Style of Your Church,* by Philip D. Douglass, PhD.

BUILDING BLOCKS OF CHURCH PERSONALITY

Each question in the diagnostic, taken by some of the leaders of **First Church Sample**, contains two opposite ideas that relate to the types of behaviors or traits of these leaders. The questions were answered according to the church leaders' preference of interaction and leadership, rather than how the church leaders think they should behave as they relate to one another and others in the church. Here is a sample of the questions:

INFORMATION GATHERING

1. Do the church leaders depend on their direct observations in order to gather evidence about what is happening in the church, or do they rely more on their innovative and general impressions in order to form a sense about what is occurring?

---

[1] *Significant portions of this report were designed and are copyrighted by Dr. Phillip Douglass, professor of applied theology and Philip and Rebecca Douglass Chair of Church Planting and Christian Formation at Covenant Theological Seminary.*

2. Do the church leaders prefer straightforward ways of communicating—the more specific and concrete the better—or do they prefer to use imagery and symbolism to engage the imagination of the people of the church?

3. Are the leaders of the church observers of tradition who do not easily break with custom, or are they able to break with tradition and lay aside customs that seem too cumbersome for a new situation?

DECISION MAKING

1. Are the church leaders secure in basing their decisions on objective, rational analysis—weighing the pros and cons of a situation in a logical fashion—or, regardless of the pros and cons, are they more confident when they feel their conclusions are based on what is important and valuable to the people of the church?

2. Can the church leaders usually get on with their work and ministry, regardless of relational harmony, or do they find that harmonious relationships are essential for them to function effectively in a situation?

3. Does making a critical evaluation occur more naturally for the church leaders than speaking an appreciative word, or are they more spontaneous with an appreciative word than with a critical evaluation?

MINISTRY STYLE

1. Do the church leaders prefer to plan their work then work their plan, or do they tend to be more casual and informal in developing their plans?

2. Do the basic contributions by the leaders often stem from being systematic, orderly, proactive, and decisive, or do they bring to church leadership such characteristics as spontaneity, open mindedness, tolerance, and adaptability?

3. Do the church leaders prefer bringing programs and projects to

completion—finishing one task at a time—or do they like the feeling of getting new things started and having many things going at the same time?

COMMUNICATION PREFERENCES ACCORDING TO CHURCH PERSONALITY
(First Church Style in Gray)

INFORMATION-GATHERING:
PRACTICAL VS. INNOVATIVE CHURCHES

Practically oriented churches pay more attention to facts, details, and current reality. Innovation is the preference of working with information on the basis of its meaningfulness, originality, and future possibilities. The most common distinctives between Practical Churches and Innovative Churches are:

PRACTICAL CHURCHES ARE INFLUENCED BY LEADERS WHO:	INNOVATIVE CHURCHES ARE INFLUENCED BY LEADERS WHO:
• live in the "here and now" • work well with facts and details • like realistic challenges and problem solving • are experience and action-oriented • are realistic and matter-of-fact	• prefer to live in the past and future • are interested in new and unusual experiences • do not like routine • are attracted to theory rather than practice

DECISION-MAKING:
ANALYTICAL VS. CONNECTIONAL CHURCHES

Analytical Churches are more likely to deal with information on the basis of its structure and function. Connectional Churches interact with information on the basis of its potential for enhancing relationships. The most common distinctives between Analytical and Connectional Churches are the following:

ANALYTICAL CHURCHES ARE INFLUENCED BY LEADERS WHO:	CONNECTIONAL CHURCHES ARE INFLUENCED BY LEADERS WHO:
• are interested in systems, structures, patterns • like to expose issues to logical analysis • can be aloof and unemotional • are likely to evaluate issues through their intellect and decide on the basis of right wrong • may have difficulty talking about emotions • may not work as diligently at clearing up arguments or quarrels	• are interested in people and their feelings • easily communicate their moods to others • pay attention to relationships • tend to evaluate issues through their ethical system and decide on the basis of good/bad • can be sensitive to rebuke • may tend to give compliments to please people

LIFESTYLE:
STRUCTURED VS. FLEXIBLE CHURCHES

Structured Churches are motivated into action proactively on the basis of advanced planning. Flexible Churches are easily motivated into action through responding to changes in events. The most common distinctives between Structured and Flexible Churches are these:

STRUCTURED CHURCHES ARE INFLUENCED BY LEADERS WHO:	FLEXIBLE CHURCHES ARE INFLUENCED BY LEADERS WHO:
• do not like to leave many unanswered questions • are likely to plan their work ahead and finish it in a timely fashion • make an effort to be exact in what they do • do not like to change their decisions once they are made • are likely to demonstrate stable work habits • easily follow rules and discipline	• may act impulsively in their ministry • can do more things at once without feeling compelled to finish them • prefer to be free from long-term obligations • are curious and like taking a fresh look at things • are likely to work according to their mood • often act without as much preparation

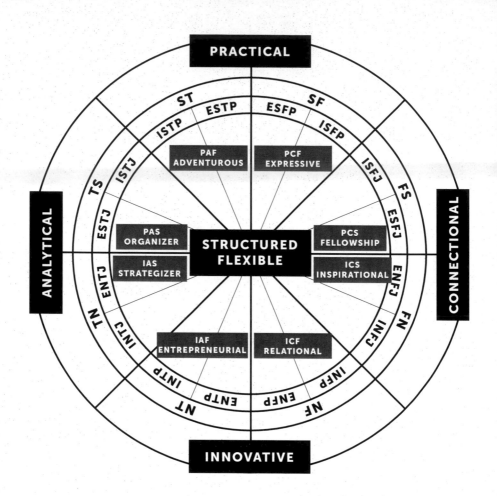

COMMUNICATION PREFERENCES
ACCORDING TO CHURCH PERSONALITY

Primary Relational / *Secondary* Expressive

FELLOWSHIP	INSPIRATIONAL	RELATIONAL	ENTREPRENEURIAL
Acts resolutely to develop and administer structures of the church that provide for the spiritual, emotional, mental, physical, and social needs of people. Values are drawn from scriptural teachings about the true needs of people in the context of their particular community.	Supplies the inspiration and organization to encourage and energize the people of the church and community to be all they can be in First Church Sample. Values clear insights into the people of the church and community that provide a multi-faceted vision for the future.	Energetically and enthusiastically envisions and communicates exciting opportunities for people from a scriptural point of view. Filters everything through a consistent core of values based on respect for the needs of individuals in their church and community.	Searches the church and community for inspiring ideas and energizing possibilities that advance the mission of the church in accordance with scriptural values. Logically structures a variety of insights into systems of thought to better understand world and lead the church more effectively.
STRATEGIZER	ORGANIZER	ADVENTUROUS	EXPRESSIVE
Leads the people of the church decisively while organizing the ministry to accomplish long-term objectives derived from scriptural teaching. Values clear insights into the structures of the church that provide present and future opportunities for accomplishing the mission.	Resolutely, rationally, and effectively organizes and leads the church to attain God-honoring goals. Values and depends on gathering facts about the events impacting the church and world from a scriptural world and life view.	Recognizes and appreciates the wide diversity within the church and world while spontaneously ministering to it. Logically structures and acts on large amounts of specific facts from scripture about the material aspects of the church's mission.	Energized by relating to people in ways that appreciate and make use of their diversity of experience. Directed by scriptural values that respect and serve both the people of the church and the community.

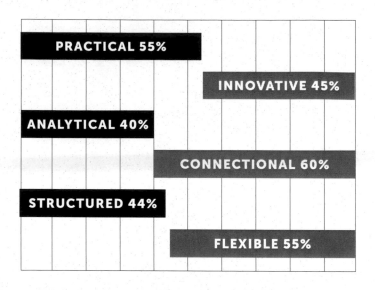

PRACTICAL 55%

INNOVATIVE 45%

ANALYTICAL 40%

CONNECTIONAL 60%

STRUCTURED 44%

FLEXIBLE 55%

CHARACTERISTICS OF THE RELATIONAL MINISTRY STYLE

(Primary Church Style)

	FIRST CHURCH	ALTERNATIVE STYLE
The way First Church takes in information	**Innovative** Churches that prefer innovation tend to take in information from patterns and the big picture as well as focus on future possibilities.	**Practical** Churches that prefer practicality tend to take in information through the five senses and focus on the here and now.
The way First Church makes decisions	**Connectional** Churches that focus on connections tend to make decisions based primarily on values and on subjective evaluation of person-centered concerns.	**Analytical** Churches that prefer analysis tend to make decisions based primarily on logic and on objective examination of cause and effect.
How First Church deals with the outer world	**Flexible** Churches that prefer flexibility tend to appreciate an adaptable and spontaneous approach to life.	**Structured** Churches that prefer structure tend to like a planned and organized approach to life and prefer to have things settled.

MEMBER INTERACTION SCALE

Church member interaction style impacts both the manner in which the church's opinion leaders minister together and how well they minister together.

There is a **moderately high degree of agreement** between the **methods** and **evidence** validated in the decision-making process. While Practical types have a slight majority over Innovative types, the pastor's propensity toward innovation gives greater day-to-day emphasis on innovation. Also, Flexible types tend to be more comfortable with ambiguity over Structured types, giving the overall dominance to a preference for Innovation and Flexibility over Practicality and Structure.

The Presbyterian Church in America (PCA) is a Practical, Analytical, Structured (PAS) organization. Our polity places emphasis upon absolute clarity over ambiguity, on form and process over relational interaction, and structure. Thus, PAS-style leaders are over-represented within sessions across the denomination. Finding great commonality, the PCS types make up the secondary type denomination wide. However, taking into account sociological factors, the PCS church is the most common organizing style within the denomination, with PAS being the second most common. Flexible organizations are prone to limited scalability by the lack of structure.

Over time, and with particularization, the PCA polity will draw First Church Sample toward a PAS style. The demological preferences of the community will draw First Church Sample toward PCS. Some of the indications of these structural, connectional values will reflect in "relational fatigue," or the seeming inability of members to make room for new visitors; a focus on the church building as the center for congregational life and activity; and the propensity to begin in-reaching ministries (i.e., events that draw outsiders into the church building for interaction).

Innovative types need to give room for Practical types to push—even "challenge"—vision and direction in order to develop concrete trust in the vision. At the same time, Practical types should not be allowed to refuse movement or grow rigid in the absence of desired concrete information. Rather, Practical types should draw out the factual data behind the Innovative approach through open-ended questions and non-anxious engagement.

Next, a **low degree of agreement** with the over-representation of the Connectional type is common when looking at the data from Claritas® (pgs. 13–15). Any combination of lower income, non-white, and younger populations tend toward Connectional preferences over Analytical preferences. It is important that the under-represented Analytical types be allowed to strive for objective standards of truth and a "tough-minded" approach of treating everybody equally, despite the Connectional propensity to strive for harmony and positive interactions and a "tenderhearted" approach of treating everyone as an individual. At this stage in the organizing process, this is the potentially the greatest source of conflict.

Finally, there is a **moderately low degree of agreement** between the structures necessary for the perceived health of the organization. Classic among young churches is a high degree of Flexibility with regard to organizing structure. However, as organizations move toward greater cohesion, they move toward a more structured approach. I believe this is represented in the 55/45 split between Flexibility and Structure.

HOW YOUR RELATIONAL-STYLE MEMBERS APPROACH CONFLICT

Because the Relational (ICF) component is strong, it is worth looking at how this style also approaches conflict. This is further insightful because of the increased level of difference between the Relational and Expressive styles of ministry.

INTUITIVE
- Ponders every opportunity
- Considers all the options
- Works at many issues simultaneously
- Reflects on what lies ahead
- Analyzes movements and developments
- Envisions what is possible

CONNECTIONAL
- Includes everyone to solve problems
- Cares about impact of actions on people
- Applies ideals to decision making
- Solicits involvement from members
- Labors to maintain peace in the church

ANALYTICAL
- Investigates
- Scrutinizes
- Deliberate
- Debates basic suppositions
- Develops or employs a paradigm
- Organizes information logically

PRACTICAL
- Searches for information pertinent to the problem
- Recognizes appropriate boundaries
- Effectively implements plans
- Formulates step by step solutions
- Resists novel methods

If the schedule allows one hour, your **Relational** Church will prefer to allocate its time this way:

30 MINUTES
considering pondering every option to envision future potential

18 MINUTES
considering relational issues in decision making

9 MINUTES
gathering data and forming step-by-step plans

3 MINUTES
organizing information and analyzing basic suppositions

HOW YOUR EXPRESSIVE-STYLE MEMBERS APPROACH CONFLICT

Because the Expressive (PCF) component is strong, it is worth looking at how this style also approaches conflict. This is further insightful because of the increased level of difference between the Expressive and Relational styles of ministry.

CONNECTIONAL

- Includes everyone to solve problems
- Cares about impact of actions on people
- Applies ideals to decision making
- Solicits involvement from members
- Labors to maintain peace in the church

PRACTICAL

- Searches for information pertinent to the problem
- Recognizes appropriate boundaries
- Effectively implements plans
- Formulates step by step solutions
- Resists novel methods

INTUITIVE

- Ponders every opportunity
- Considers all the options
- Works at many issues simultaneously
- Reflects on what lies ahead
- Analyzes movements and developments
- Envisions what is possible

ANALYTICAL

- Investigates
- Scrutinizes
- Deliberate
- Debates basic suppositions
- Develops or employs a paradigm
- Organizes information logically

If the schedule allows one hour, your **Expressive** Church will prefer to allocate its time this way:

30 MINUTES
considering relational issues in decision making

18 MINUTES
gathering data and forming step-by-step plans

9 MINUTES
considering pondering every option to envision future potential

3 MINUTES
organizing information and analyzing basic suppositions

CHURCH PROFILE: SELF-ASSESSMENT

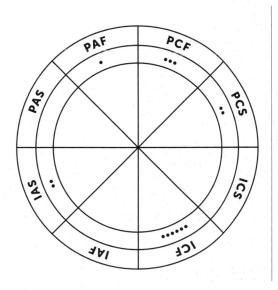

PRIMARY STYLE:
Relational
SECONDARY STYLE:
Expressive

LEGEND
PAF = ADVENTUROUS
PCF = EXPRESSIVE
PCS = FELLOWSHIP
ICS = INSPIRATIONAL
ICF = RELATIONAL
IAF = ENTREPRENEURIAL
IAS = STRATEGIZER
PAS = ORGANIZER

IN-REACH VS. OUT-REACH

There are two different ways to do ministry. Both are needful and both valid. You cannot have just one, but every church emphasizes one over the other.

Churches that emphasize In-Reach need the structure of the physical church space to create opportunities for relationship, teaching, and evangelism. These churches depend upon the structure that the actual location provides. Ministry isn't primarily "out there" but "in here." The church building is often the draw: *"Let's get them in here to hear the truth and see how loving we are."* Like Israel before the exile, "If we do faithfully what God has called us to do, people will come in." These churches often have midweek events at the church, may prefer clearly defined events like VBS or a Christmas music program, and often start schools.

Churches that emphasize Out-Reach typically push events, engagements, and ministry opportunities away from the church. These churches prefer the flexibility that other venues provide. Ministry isn't primarily "in here" but "out there." The event is the draw: *Let's get out there to engage with people so they can hear the truth and see how loving we are.*" Like the great commission, "Go therefore and make disciples of all the nations, baptizing them in the name of the Father and of the Son and of the Holy Spirit."

IS FIRST CHURCH SAMPLE IN-REACH OR OUT-REACH?

I do not have enough data to determine where First Church Sample falls in this regard.

COMMUNITY PERSONALITY

BACKGROUND ON CLARITAS RESULTS

Claritas® is an arm of Nielson Research, presenting demographic and socio-economic data by zip code. Intended for use by companies, we have applied this data to organizational style in order to show common organizing elements between a church and the local community. We ran comparative analysis of thriving churches in known markets, using fundamental organizing principles, and adjusted for the propensity of self-selection. Using the Myers Briggs Type Indicator (MBT) as a framework, we have been able to match Claritas® Social Groups to corresponding church and individual typological preferences.

UNDERSTANDING CLARITAS® RESULTS

A church should look for consistency and overlap in its own Church Personality style and that of the corresponding community. Where there is similarity, questions should be asked about capitalizing on existing models of ministry in order to engage the community. Where there is dissimilarity, questions should be asked about necessary adjustments to existing models of ministry in order to reach the community. Primarily, we are looking for significant discrepancies in style and preference between First Church Sample and the immediate community.

FIRST CHURCH SAMPLE AND COMMUNITY

The following are characteristics of the area immediately surrounding First Church Sample. While churches regularly draw from a 10-mile radius, growing churches maintain significant overlap between their models of ministry and the organizing values of the immediate community.

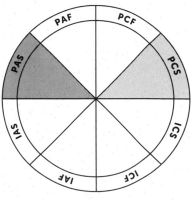

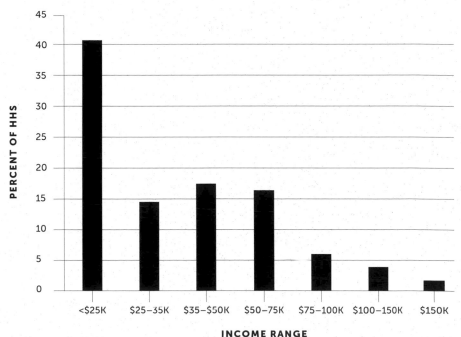

HOUSEHOLDS BY INCOME

FIRST CHURCH SAMPLE AND COMMUNITY

HOUSEHOLD COMPOSITION

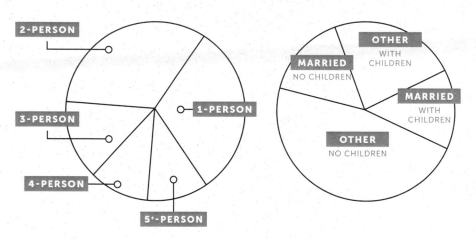

POPULATION BY AGE

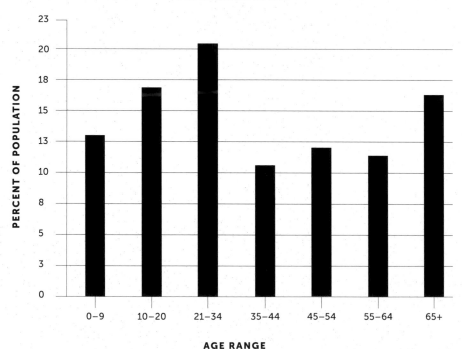

FIRST CHURCH SAMPLE AND COMMUNITY

POPULATION BY RACE & ETHNICITY

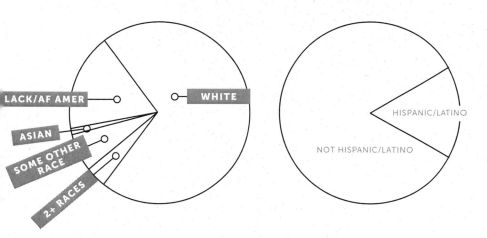

Sample Job Description — Senior Pastor

This **Senior Pastor Profile and Information Packet** is designed to share our ministry opportunity and to seek those who might be interested in exploring a call to serve with us. Please review the packet and reflect on the role and required skills, and work to discern whether this ministry would be right for you or someone you know.

Our congregation has grown in its identity as a church, summarized in the categories of worship, discipleship, outreach, and missions.

- Our primary expression of outreach is church planting, and our members embrace church planting as a part of who we are and what we do. Our weekly attendance and membership over the years fluctuated as new churches were sent out. In 2013, our congregation planted two new churches, and we desire to replenish the size of our congregation. God has continued to be faithful in bringing new families into our fellowship.

- Today our congregation is one of the largest churches in our Presbytery. Our current active involvement exceeds 450, and our general fund giving for the ministry year just concluded was $970,000.

CHURCH PROFILE

Our congregation demographically reflects the community and the surrounding area. Our congregation has a growing number of families with young children. Of the 80 families currently attending our church with children (0–18 yrs.), 52 have children 12 and under, totaling 117 children under 12.

The greater metropolitan area has a population of 2,138,038, which is the largest in our state and the twenty-seventh most populous in the U.S. Our city is a family-friendly city with significant arts, culture, religion, values, and architecture that stem from its multicultural immigrant beginnings. Recent developments include upgrades to the _____. Sports teams include _____. Notable educational institutions include the University _____. The business community is thriving, with 15 Fortune 1000 companies. Several of our church plants are located in the greater metropolitan area.

Our congregation is located in an outer suburb of the greater metropolitan area, close to two major interstates. Most residents live within approximately a 20–25-minute drive to downtown.

COMMUNITY PROFILE

Our community was recently ranked as the seventh-best place to live by a national magazine, primarily due to its schools, amenities, and businesses. Our public schools consistently perform among the best in the state, placing fifth out of 613 state school districts in 2010. Our community is also home to several public golf courses, a water park, Kings Island amusement park, and _____.

Our community has changed dramatically over the last 20 years. Originally a small farming community, today the city covers about 18 square miles and is home to more than 31,000 people and approximately 500 businesses, _____, _____, and _____.

As the community has developed, its demographics have also diversified. According to a recent study, currently 1 in 4 elementary students is non-Anglo. This presents an exciting opportunity for our church and its ministry to the families God has brought to our area.

MISSION AND VISION STATEMENT

Our Vision: The vision of our congregation is to be a "City on a Hill," proclaiming the gospel in word and deed to the metropolitan area and the world. The image of the City on a Hill is taken from Jesus's words in Matthew 5:14, "You are the light of the world. A city on a hill cannot be hidden," which describes the role of the church in the world. A city is a place of resources, refuge, community, and hope, and our goal is to offer the same blessings to those around us.

Our Mission: We strive to become a City on a Hill by:
- Worshipping God in spirit and truth,
- Making mature disciples of Christ, and
- Reaching a needy world through missions, mercy ministry, evangelism, and church planting.

Our Values: Worshipping God is our highest value. Sunday morning worship services are a vital part of our ministry. In our services, we seek to glorify God, edify the believer, and be sensitive to those still learning about Christ. Our worship style is a combination of contemporary and traditional, and God's Word is our guide. Our goal is to honor God and encourage people to draw closer to him.

MAJOR CHURCH PROGRAMS AND COMMITTEES

Our ministry philosophy follows the scriptural perspective expounded in *The Trellis and the Vine,* by Colin Marshall and Tony Pane. Programs enable "life-on-life" ministry, and we favor "vine work" of discipleship over "trellis work" of programs. One aspect of the pastor's job description is to be a leader/equipper for the congregation.

Our congregation's major programs and events include:

- Men's Discipleship Network
- Women's Joy Ministry
- Life Groups
- Interfaith Hospitality Network
- Global Missions Team
- Hospitality Team

STAFF AND LEADERSHIP TEAM

One of the hallmarks of our church has always been the fellowship and team atmosphere of our staff. Our staff enjoys healthy balance of connectedness, communication through weekly staff meetings and quarterly dinners, and also the freedom to develop our ministries within the appropriate means of accountability.

Pastoral and Program Staff:

_____ – Senior Pastor

_____ – Associate Pastor / Director of Christian Formation

_____ – Worship Director

_____ – Children's Ministry Director

_____ – Nursery Director

Office and Support Staff:

_____ – Office Manager

_____ – Communications Director

_____ – Bookkeeper

_____ – Facilities Manager

OPEN POSITION AND QUALIFICATIONS

After years of dedicated service, our senior pastor announced his desire to make a career transition from the senior pastor role and began working with the session on a search and succession plan. He will continue serving as the senior pastor through January 2017. Our pastors, staff, session, and congregational relationships are strong, loving, and mature, enabling us to initiate an orderly transition to a new senior pastor who has a passion to lead our congregation forward.

God has given us members, resources, leadership, and a desire to achieve a higher level of impact in the community. We would like our senior pastor to lead us to set and prioritize specific long-term goals in the following areas:

- Numerical growth
- Facilities expansion and campus development
- Church planting
- Life-on-life discipleship

The following describes more fully the senior pastor role and the philosophy, behaviors, and traits that we desire in prospective candidates for this position.

SENIOR PASTOR ROLE:

- *Vision:* Originate vision, mission, and ministry plans. Get input and secure ownership.
- *Leadership:* Lead vision, mission, and ministry plans. Execution of vision, mission, ministry plan through staff and congregation.
- *Ministry:* Develop ministry programs to accomplish vision, mission, ministry plans. Equip saints. Develop leadership.
- *Management:* Lead staff, periodically evaluate accomplishments for contribution to ministry plan and stated goals.

BEHAVIORS

- **Leadership:** Vision setting, engages to share, helps people understand, and helps accomplish.
- **Teaching:** Bible focused, application oriented, and willingness to speak the truth.
- **Counsel:** Prayerful, compassionate, wisdom oriented (personal and biblical).
- **Humility:** A servant leader, collaborative, and respected.
- **Connected:** Knows the body, listens, has awareness of what is happening, shepherds the flock.
- **Discipleship:** Exhibits a daily walk with the Lord and seeks to help others to do the same.
- **Change:** Is willing to alter paths; helps bring others on the journey when change is required; is not inhibited by knowing there will be disagreement.

THEOLOGY AND ECCLESIOLOGY

- Commitment to theology as defined in the PCA standards.
- Appreciation for the broader body of Christ and willing to partner with other ministries.
- Theologically astute and discerning.
- Understands issues in the PCA.
- Not drawn to controversy.
- Respected for convictions.
- Speaks the truth in love.

PERSONAL TRAITS

- Discerning, wise, mature demeanor.
- Skilled in biblical conflict resolution.
- Integrity, humility.
- Sets and communicates vision effectively.
- Winsome, personable, engaging.

GIFTS AND ABILITIES

- Strong preaching gifts required (more than teaching gifts).
- Able to originate and lead vision, mission, and ministry plans.
- Administratively proficient.
- Able to select, lead, and develop associate/assistant pastors and staff.
- Solid written and oral communication skills and the ability to inspire and influence people.
- Leadership presence both in one-on-one situations and in large group settings.

EXPERIENCE AND EDUCATION

- Master of Divinity (MDiv) required.
- Five or more years of pastoral ministry experience in a church setting.
- Significant preaching experience.
- Proven ability to gather and grow a community.
- Experience exercising oversight for a large body in a church setting.
  + Preferably a senior pastor or assistant/associate pastor in church of 100+.
  + Experience in more than one congregation desirable.
- Experience supervising others desirable.
- Member of the PCA in good standing.

PHILOSOPHY OF MINISTRY / MISSION, VISION, VALUES

The successful candidate must be motivated by a vision to maintain our congregational core distinctives while advancing areas in which we desire to grow or reexamine. See chart on next page.

CORE DISTINCTIVES

- Balance of traditional and contemporary worship—informal business casual
- Evangelism through church planting and mentoring new ministers
- Active work in global missions and home missions
- Life-on-life discipleship
- Winsomely Reformed
    + Intellectually and culturally relevant
    + Reasonable; not unnecessarily offensive
    + Appreciative of contributions of greater body of Christ

DESIRED GROWTH

- Worship that glorifies God, edifies the believer, and evangelizes the unchurched
- A magnetism, community vision, and energy that draw the community into worship
- Grow to become a body of 800–1200
- Local outreach, community involvement, and mercy ministry
- Music and the arts (as outreach and worship)

AREAS TO EXPLORE

- Re-examination of vision to update, clarify, and improve upon
- Avoid becoming a program church with "too much trellis"
- Ministry that embraces modern use of communications and technology

Sample Behavioral Interviewing Questions

1. First Presbyterian Church has experience with hardship. Describe a time you shepherded hurting people through a particularly difficult situation. What was the process you took them through? How did you describe and shepherd the grieving process with these people?

2. Where there are two or more people, there is a tendency to conflict. Describe a time you had conflict with another person (outside your marriage). Describe as best you can, without naming names, the situation. How did you engage the people involved? What was the outcome of your interactions over this issue?

3. The term "shepherding" can have different, if not equally biblical, expressions. Using a specific situation in your most recent ministry, describe how you approach shepherding with an average congregant. What steps were involved? How did you define the objectives of the interaction with the congregant? What were some of the outcomes? What have you learned from such interactions?

4. First Presbyterian Church has fairly strong in-reach structures in place. We also recognize the need for outreach into our community, businesses, and neighborhoods. Describe for us a situation in your recent ministry where you helped a group of people grow in their ability to engage with people outside their immediate relational context. What steps did you take? What was the response? What did you learn?

5. The First Presbyterian Church community is very family focused, with emphasis on education and the outdoors (sports, hiking, etc.). At the same time, the community is very diverse socio-economically. At First Pres, we seek to reach the un-churched and de-churched across the entire community. Describe a time you tried to make in roads and connections with people who were different from you. Describe what you hoped to accomplish and what the outcomes were.

6. We anticipate First Presbyterian Church moving toward particularization in the PCA in the near future. This move will have many different aspects that will fall within the responsibilities of the pastor and many different aspects that will fall within the responsibilities of different members of the body. Describe a time you were part of significant change in an organization. What was your role? Describe the steps you took to engage with all the parties involved. Describe specifically what elements of change you led and which elements were delegated. What was the outcome of that change?

7. First Presbyterian practices a traditional approach to musical components, augmented with several blended-style components (e.g., guitar, drums, Indelible Grace hymns). Describe a time you had to lead or direct a group of people with varied musical styles toward a unified worship service. What happened? What were the results? What did you learn?

8. First Presbyterian Church recently celebrated the retirement of its founding pastor. This was a period of joy and sadness. Tell us about a time you helped a group of people dealing with a variety of emotions connected to the same event. How did you identify the

different emotions? How did you help people connect with others who had different feelings? What did you learn?

9. We live in a highly sexualized culture. Our view is that nobody has escaped that unscathed. Thinking about a time when you were tempted sexually, tell us about how you sought purity and sobriety in the midst of that temptation.

ENDNOTES

Friedman, Edwin. *Failure of Nerve*. Seabury Books, 2007.

Spurgeon, A., C. A. Jackson, and J. R. Beach, "The Life Events Inventory: Re-Scaling Based on an *Occupational Sample*," Occupational Medicine 51, no. 4 (2001): 287–93.

ABOUT THE AUTHOR

Joel Hathaway is the son of a pastor who served in the Bible Presbyterian Church, the Presbyterian Church in America, and, most recently, the Associate Reformed Presbyterian Church. Joel holds a bachelor of arts in English from the University of Alabama, and a master of divinity and doctor of ministry from Covenant Theological Seminary. His doctoral research studied assistant pastors who served as the interim pastors of their congregations during a senior-leadership transition. For the last decade, he has served as director of alumni and career services for Covenant Seminary. Joel is married to Shannon, and they have four children.